W9-CNP-252

THE $ENSIBLE $AVER®

*A Commonsense Guide to Saving More
While Still Living Well*

THE $ENSIBLE $AVER®

*A Commonsense Guide to Saving More
While Still Living Well*

by Mark W. Miller

MACMILLAN/SPECTRUM

Copyright © 1996 by $ensible $aver Publications, Inc.

All rights reserved. No part of this book shall be reproduced, stored in a retrieval system, or transmitted by any means, electronic, mechanical, photocopying, recording, or otherwise without written permission from the publisher. No patent liability is assumed with respect to the use of the information contained herein. Although every precaution has been taken in preparation of this book, the publisher and authors assume no responsibility for errors or omissions. Neither is any liability assumed for damages resulting from the use of the information contained herein. For information, address Macmillan/Spectrum, 1633 Broadway, 7th Floor, New York, NY 10019-6785.

International Standard Book Number: 0-02-861288-4

Library of Congress Cataloging Card Number: 96-068538

98 97 96   9 8 7 6 5 4 3 2

Interpretation of the printing code: the rightmost number of the first series of numbers is the year of the book's printing; the rightmost number of the second series of numbers is the number of the book's printing. For example, a printing code of 96-1 shows that the first printing occurred in 1996.

Printed in the United States of America

Reasonable care has been taken in the preparation of the text to ensure its clarity and accuracy. This book is sold with the understanding that the author and the publisher are not engaged in rendering legal, accounting, or other professional service. Laws vary from state to state, and readers with specific financial questions should seek the services of a professional advisor.

The author and the publisher specifically disclaim any liability, loss, or risk, personal or otherwise, which is incurred as a consequence, directly or indirectly, of the use and application of any of the contents of this book.

$ensible $aver publications is a solely owned corporation; Mark W. Miller, president. The $ensible $aver® is a registered trademark of $ensible $aver Publications, Inc. Any use of it in whole or part is strictly prohibited by law without the express written permission of the owner.

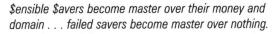

$ensible $avers become master over their money and domain . . . failed savers become master over nothing.

—Mark W. Miller

DEDICATION

This money creation is dedicated to the memory of my father, William J. Miller, whose common sense was not so common. His wisdom and inspiration were the most precious investments of capital he made in the lives of those around him.

TABLE OF CONTENTS

INTRODUCTION

Money is a guarantee that we may have what we want in the future. Though we might need nothing at the moment, it ensures the possibility of satisfying a new desire when it arises.

—Aristotle

From Desperation to Financial Reward

Six years ago, I was out of work and almost dead broke. In between jobs, I was trying to make ends meet by doing odds and ends work such as house painting. It was just enough to keep me one step *behind* my creditors. They were calling constantly, reminding me I was overdue and wondering when the money was coming. Most of my time was spent figuring out ingenious ways to keep them at bay while I tried to get my head back above water. At the time I was thousands of dollars in debt and really didn't see any way out.

I had a used 1982 Honda Accord that was rusting from the inside out. I was still driving it although the back was smashed up from an accident several months earlier. I couldn't afford to get it fixed. My family jokingly referred to it as the Honda Accordion. All I needed was a monkey on my shoulder to make the picture complete. I looked pretty stupid in it, judging from the looks received from others on the highway. The worst thing was that it wasn't even paid for. Some luck!

I lived in a cracker-box apartment with walls so thin you could smell food cooking in the apartments on either side. In the winter, drafts would roar in from just about every window. It was impossible to plug them all up. We just lived with the cold. Every couple of weeks, my roommate and I scrounged up some money and took a trip to the grocery store. We would usually come home (I use this word loosely) with a wonderful assortment of Hamburger Helper, potatoes, and beans. This was about all, and I'm still amazed that we were able to subsist on such a diet. Needless to say, life was pretty bad.

Even worse than the physical conditions were the feelings I had about myself and where I was headed. I was clueless as to how I would get myself out of this mess and bounce back to where I had been a few years earlier when I was a financial planner. That's right, I was supposed to be an expert on personal finances! How could I have gotten into such a mess? Actually, I always knew the formulas and strategies for financial success very well; I just wasn't using them. The plans were in my head; I just had to figure out a way to put them into action. I decided that if I was going to do anything significant in the future I had to make a commitment to the one person I had been neglecting for quite some time: myself.

I sat down and mapped out a strategy for saving and investing for the next several years. At the time, I wanted so much it seemed impossible to foresee that I could accomplish everything. I wanted to build a four-bedroom, 2,500-square-foot house overlooking a lake. I wanted a new car, or at least a car that ran well and didn't shake every time you pulled up to a stop sign. I definitely wanted to go on a Caribbean cruise and a tour of Europe. Most of all, I wanted to be able to pay the bills and not have to constantly worry about money. That was a lot of goals, and I was naive enough to think they could be accomplished in five years!

I wrote all my goals down on paper and tacked them up everywhere around my apartment. Then I began to develop a plan of attack. I decided to devote more time to painting houses until I could find better work. The pay wasn't the best, but I knew I could work around that by freeing up money in other ways from the tricks I had learned when I was a financial planner. I developed a method called "Bill Myself" to automatically start saving money. The plan was simple and didn't involve being tied to a budget day in and day out (see Chapter 3). I also figured a way to start paying off my creditors and keep them from pounding down the door. I started really watching what I was spending and evaluating whether it would get me closer to the goals I had set. Above all, I thought and struggled every day about some of the most important things in my financial life. I began to become passionate about what I was going to do in the future.

About two and a half years into my new life, I took a serious look at my progress and was amazed at the distance I had traveled. I had gone from being in tremendous debt with not a penny to my name, to having many of my creditors paid off and over $20,000 in the bank! By the third year I had saved about $25,000 and took that Caribbean cruise I had planned. I also got the nice car I so desperately wanted. By the fourth year, I had built the house of my dreams and also put $40,000 in the bank, one year behind schedule. What about Europe? I went on an exotic trip to Greece and Turkey that will never be forgotten. In case you're wondering, all of this was accomplished on a moderate income. What is most incredible about the journey is that I was able to save so much and still enjoy a lifestyle that was even better than before.

I don't tell you all this to impress you; the fact of the matter is that it impresses me! To know that these strategies and techniques work so well is amazing. By applying a little discipline and most of all, know-how, anyone can turn their financial life around in a very short time just like I did.

Early in the saving game, I began writing down many of the strategies and techniques I was using so I could follow them more closely and have some good records. For years, people had asked me how they could best manage their money. They even asked me when I was broke! (A word of advice . . . only ask a person who has money about money. Back then, I would have given you a theory I had learned and never practiced; now I can give you facts.) I would have thought most people would want to know where to invest money. However, most of the questions were about how to free up money to invest for the future. The fact is, most people need to know how to make more money and find extra money they might be throwing away before they can even begin to invest in the first place.

It finally dawned on me one day that, since I was fortunate enough to have so much success with my saving adventures, maybe others could benefit too. That's when *The $ensible Saver* newsletter was born (see the back of this book for subscription information).

I began working on the newsletter in early 1993, and launched the first issue in January of 1994. It took a while, but eventually it was noticed nationally and has been featured in major newspapers and magazines across the country. I have appeared on dozens of radio and television programs talking about the saving revolution that is sweeping the country based on the principles of *The $ensible $aver.* My savings philosophies even garnered me a invitation to Washington, D.C. to visit with top government officials, and I received a letter of commendation from the President. I can't think of any institution that needs the savings techniques I teach more than our government!

I feel fortunate to be able to help people get out from under the pressures of the almighty buck. It is sad we live in a country that is full of messages on how to consume but so few on how to provide and save for the future. Be that as it may, we still live in a country that allows us the opportunity to control circumstances around us and take responsibility into our own hands. I know that everyone, no matter what background they come from, has the freedom to strike out on their own and change their life for the better. My money techniques are solid and can be applied to just about every area of your personal finances. They are, of course, "sensible," and you don't have to be a money guru to start using them right away. Use this book wisely and you will definitely enhance the quality of your life.

How to Read This Book for Maximum Success

There have been a lot of books written about saving money, and I've personally read a boatload of them. When I first began to write *The $ensible $aver,* I wanted to write a book that was a different from—and better than—all the rest.

Many personal finance and saving books are preachy and never give simple and practical ways for you to change your habits. Often, the books give you so many ideas and theories that you're thoroughly confused. When you're reading, you think to yourself, "Wow, that's a great idea," only to forget it ten seconds later when you read the next great idea.

Don't get me wrong; *The $ensible $aver* is jam-packed with information on saving for your future, but the last thing I want is for you to read this book and forget what you've read as soon as you put it down. That's why I've included an "action list" at the end of each chapter to help you implement the most important concepts. This book is not meant to be read and digested in one short sitting. It is the type of book you will have to read several times in order to take full advantage of its money powers. After you read it for the first time, keep it close by so that you can refer to it if you ever get stuck in a financial rut and need a quick fix.

Some of the tips and strategies I talk about can be implemented right away, but others will take time to become a part of your life. The way I see it is that I could throw you a bunch of facts and theories, and then let you attack them willy-nilly and hope some of them stick. Or, I could take a much more effective approach. I'm sure you have heard the fisherman's story from the Bible. If you give a man a fish, you will feed him for a day, but if you teach a man to fish, you will feed him for a lifetime. Same thing here. I prefer to teach and guide you along the path to financial freedom and not just throw you a few tasty pieces of tuna. So take your time reading this book, and as you do, think about the fish story. Learn and absorb.

The $ensible $aver is divided into three parts:

- Part I, **Developing Lifetime Saving Habits,** consists of great saving philosophies that have helped me to become successful at saving.

- Part II, **Tips and Strategies to Save a Bundle,** is filled with lots of simple-to-implement tips and strategies that will help you free up hundreds, even thousands, of dollars you thought you never had.

- Part III, **$ensible Money Management,** gives you some general guidelines to control your money once you have accumulated a healthy nest egg.

I suggest you read *The $ensible $aver* three times. You may be thinking, "Right, three times. I don't possibly have that kind of time." Well, you need to make the time if you want to save thousands. Read it the first time without stopping to implement the ideas and strategies right away. Just get through it. The second time, read with a highlighter and mark all the most important points. You can then start to use the strategies to your best benefit. Also, this is when you should begin to use the action lists. The last time you read it, pay special attention to the highlighted areas and watch for things you missed in previous readings.

I will guarantee the following if you stick to this plan of reading:

1. No matter how many times you read the book, you will come away with a new concept each time.

2. You will be much more educated about your personal finances and will even be able to educate others on several money concepts.

3. You will have maximum success in your financial life.

I've tried to write this book just like I write my newsletter, in a conversational tone. I will repeat very important ideas in this book several times. This is because I feel repetition is very helpful. Frankly, I think people are fed up with stuffy Wall Street jargon about money, so I try to bring the language down to earth and make things easy to understand. Think of this as a conversation between you and me. I promise to talk *with* you rather than preach *at* you.

Your part of the conversation is taking action to improve your financial life. You can have all the knowledge in the world about money, but if you sit on your behind, you're not going to accomplish anything. Knowledge isn't power until it's combined with action. I challenge you to become what I call an "action buck." This is a dollar that doesn't just collect dust under some mattress, but is constantly out there churning up the waters of the economy and recruiting other dollars to come along for the ride. Go out there and start attracting more dollars through active participation!

One last important point. I honestly want this book to help you get more out of your life. I've learned enough about money to realize that it's not evil, as some may think. It's simply a means to obtain more freedom in life. I have a rather lofty purpose for my life that I would like to share with you that goes beyond just accumulating cash:

> *From this day forward, I commit myself to*
> *helping one million people in the world unleash*
> *their true potential and realize greater*
> *personal, professional, and financial freedom.*
> *I won't stop until it's done!*

Will you join me in making this a reality? Have a great time reading *The $ensible $aver!*

To your lifelong success,

PART I

Developing Lifetime Saving Habits

CHAPTER 1

Financial Independence Without Settling for Less

> I have found most people don't understand emotional economics. That is, they can't grasp the concept that money is not just an object with which we buy things, but a complex system that can allow our lives to expand and grow for the better.
>
> —*Mark W. Miller*

Learning the Value of a Dollar

My second year into college, I had about $6,000 in a savings account I was just itching to spend. I was fixated on a sharp sapphire-blue Camaro that I felt was a great investment. My father had other ideas. He sat me down and tried his best to explain to me the value of a dollar and especially the value of $6,000.

My father grew up in a small Missouri town outside Kansas City called Liberty. When he was young, not many people in Liberty had much money. It was a town of hard-working folks who definitely knew the value of a buck. My father was brought up in a family that saved as much as it could and took a vacation only once in a while. It was in this environment that he learned to respect people's opinions on money and gain their trust to handle it for them. At a young age, he took a job as a teller with a large bank in Kansas City and worked his way up to be a vice president. He then began to invest in several profitable community banks throughout the state of Missouri. He attained this stature primarily because of his ability to get along with others and his small-town common sense about money. For years, we lived a far more comfortable life than he was accustomed to growing up in Liberty. Living in the nice part of Kansas City, we were never short of money.

My father wanted me to hold onto the $6,000 I had socked away for college expenses, but as a college student, I wasn't thinking about saving. I bought the sporty car, and it turned out that he was right. I had a rough time paying for many of my college expenses that year. Our arrangement was he paid for tuition, room and board, and I paid for all the incidentals. Those incidentals sure did add up. When I went to my father on my knees asking for money to help, he didn't give me any. Every time I got into the car, I felt guilty. . . guilty enough to finally sell it for a hefty loss.

If my father taught me anything, it was that money didn't grow on trees. Money is hard to make but much easier to spend. Consequently, when you get some money, you should do your best to keep it in your pocket. Often, after you spend money, you kick yourself and want it back anyway.

When interviewers ask me why I'm qualified to talk about money, I tell them because I have been flat broke and I now have plenty of money. I have been in both places, and I like having money more than being broke. I went from the money doghouse to the penthouse fast and efficiently. What I learned in this process has been the foundation for a lifetime of financial freedom, which is what I'm about to teach you. It took me several years to learn these strategies and even longer to finally learn how to apply them. Now you can learn them in just a few hours and use them for the rest of your life. This knowledge can increase your financial consciousness; using this newly acquired knowledge can empower you to success.

A Budget Is Not the Answer

One important thing you should know is that I hate the word *budget*. I call it the nasty *B* word. In fact, I think following a day-by-day budget is absolute hogwash and should be reserved for the accountants of the world. Budgeting conjures up images of complete and utter sacrifice that focuses on the negative of *not spending* rather than the positive nature of saving to produce a better future.

Budgeting does not create a lifetime of wealth but only a lifetime of worry and doubt. A budget is actually a moneymaking killer, not a moneymaker.

This philosophy probably sounds quite a bit different from what you have been taught. You may have heard the first thing you need to do to get control of your finances is to make a budget. This advice is a bunch of rubbish. If my theory doesn't sound right, ask yourself one question: Are you rich? I rest my case.

I once heard a terrific story about a very wealthy gentleman who was the head trustee on the board of his church. For months, the church had lost money and was continually trying to find new ways to cut expenses. Every trustee meeting consisted of arguments about what should and shouldn't be cut and how to change the budget to accommodate these cuts. All the time and energy of several very bright people was consumed by the thought of bankruptcy and this wonderful church going belly up. At one meeting, this head trustee had a brilliant idea. He suggested that the trustees focus on the positive instead of spending all their time focusing on the negative.

The head trustee said to everyone, "Maybe we should be looking at ways to make more money and save on things we are already buying, instead of looking at ways to cut expenses." From that point on, the board began to focus on new programs and church functions to bring more money into the coffers. They also became more frugal when they bought needed supplies and inventory. Consequently, the church has made enough money that it is now profitable; it has even added several new charity programs that had been on the back burner for years.

The moral of this story: If your mind is stuck in the rut of money damage control or worried about the pennies you save by cutting expenses and budgeting, you will be unable to achieve financial success. Your objective is to create more money and enhance your lifestyle, not to relegate yourself to the tedium of daily pennypinching. Creating more cash is what I have learned how to do best. If you want to learn how to budget better, go talk to an accountant.

Don't get me wrong. I don't want you to get the impression you never need to think about how you are spending your money. In fact, I think it's very important to get a clear picture of where you are standing financially at certain points in your life. Therefore, I have included an income and expenses worksheet in this book. With my system, you don't need to follow a strict budget and worry day-to-day. You need to know what you are spending to figure out what you can afford to save. But shopping for groceries with a pencil and paper to ensure you stay within a specified budget on pancake syrup is not my idea of inspiration. Instead, you should focus on producing more money and saving more money.

Look to the Pros Who Have Done It Themselves

Do you think you can become a better golfer if you ask the guy at the snack bar if he knows any good tips? My experience is that when you ask someone you have just met, he or she gives you some tip from a magazine or advice they heard from someone else. You use the new tip and end up playing twice as badly as you did before. The best way to hit the ball straight and nail the putts is to play with a pro—someone who knows all the best tips and tricks because he or she has used them effectively a thousand times. A pro is the only person who can teach you the right way to play the game.

The only money professionals in this world are the ones who have made money themselves, not those who just try to skim it off the top, such as some insurance agents, stockbrokers, financial planners, and money column editors. They all have jobs, just like the rest of us. (By the way, JOB stands for Just Over Broke.) They have theories about money, but most of these people are no different from anyone else. They need to pay their bills and, in some cases, are trying desperately to get out of debt themselves, hoping to hit the lottery soon, just like you might be.

A very respected financial writer wrote a book on how to get by on $100,000 per year. He wrote the book as a joke, but believe it or not, many people are having as much trouble making it on a $100,000 per year as those making $18,000. Many of these "rich people going broke" are the same ones who give financial advice. This point proves the adage, "It's not what you make, but what you spend." Figuring out new ways to make money and spending smart are the real keys. I've done it, and I know I can teach you how to do it, too.

Don't rely solely on the advice I give you, though. You must take 100% responsibility for your money, which means you need to teach yourself as much about money as possible. Don't just read this book, read other books on personal finance and listen to audio tapes while you're driving. If you read or listen to only one personal finance book a month, you will know a heck of a lot more about your money by the end of the year.

Secrets of People Who See You as a Victim

I have done extensive research on the companies and people who have gotten rich off America's overspending. In fact, some of these people have personally shown me how they do it. "If my customers knew about these tricks, I'd be out of business real fast" is what they tell me. In your hand is the key to unlocking these secrets. The tips and strategies in this book may not make you wealthy overnight, but they can help free up thousands of dollars you thought you never had. If you use this extra money in combination with a coordinated plan, you can systematically free yourself of many financial worries in just a few short years without drastically changing your lifestyle. You will be able to obtain true financial independence; that is, whatever financial independence means to you. It may mean another $500 per month or perhaps sailing around the world on a yacht. It really means freeing yourself from the shackles money has put around your life for years and making it work for you instead of you working for it.

We have all heard the saying, "You get what you pay for." Is this always true? I don't think so. For instance, you can buy almost all the same items at the grocery store you normally do and save as much as 40% just by knowing the tricks grocery stores use to get you to pay more. Or you can save on car maintenance, home furnishings, insurance, and even luxury vacations just by knowing trade secrets the professionals use everyday.

Imagine being able to walk into a car dealership and pay $350 less than what the dealer paid for a new car, and the dealership *wants* to sell it to you at that price. What about saving $30,000 on your dream home and still getting everything you want? Would you feel comfortable saving several hundred dollars per year on auto insurance but still be fully covered? I do.

A Word of Caution: Don't Worship the Almighty Buck

We have all heard the cliché, "money doesn't buy happiness." Money can sure put a little pleasure in your life and provide a degree of comfort, but it can't buy you lasting happiness.

You may be wondering why an author devoted to the pursuit of more money is writing about what money can't buy. This book is on how to make money, but you must understand that I would have no financial independence in life if it did not include a healthy balance between work and play. I hear so many stories about people who have made money their key reason for living and working. Ironically, these people are usually the same ones who end up bankrupt both financially and emotionally. They never learned that the key to obtaining true financial independence is maintaining independence from money. This message is worth repeating:

> *The key to obtaining true financial independence is maintaining independence from money.*

In essence, the further you get from worshipping the almighty dollar, the closer you get to finding financial independence. When you value other things in life such as your vocation and family, financial independence seems to come naturally.

A recent study showed that Americans making between $15,000 and $30,000 per year said they would be happier and could fulfill all their dreams if they made between $50,000 and $60,000 per year. When people earning $60,000 per year were asked what their happiness and dream threshold was, they said they would need $125,000 per year. Everyone always needs more money, but is more money really the answer? The real test is what you do with the extra money you make. Most people immediately spend it and increase their standard of living, only to find they hit a debt ceiling again. Look back at the times in your life when you had "more." Have those times made a lasting impact on your life, or did they just dig you deeper into a hole?

We all need some luxuries—a nice vacation or a larger home—to be happy. But we need to remember that these things are only outcomes we want or need. Although you can invest money in these types of "things," they may or may not enhance the quality of your life and the lives of the people around you.

Ask yourself whether you would quit your job if a pile of money was dropped on your doorstep. Many people who have been in this situation have not quit their jobs or even changed their lifestyles much. Why invest a lifetime or even a year in a job when you are there only for the money? Your job should be a source of satisfaction in your life because it occupies the greatest portion of your existence, next to sleeping! A job should be more than just a pay-check. It should be a chance to do something well and increase your self-esteem and the well-being of those around you.

When a family crisis such as an illness occurs, money can help ease everyone through a difficult time, but even with all its powers, money can't prepare you for the pain and sadness that are part of these events. The best way to cope with crises is to have good rela-tionships with family and friends, not a pile of money.

Having both money and happiness *is* possible. The key is to strike a healthy balance between your financial life and your "life." Be very careful if your pursuit of wealth and success is driving you to the brink. Reevaluate your direction and see if you can focus on those things in life that are longer lasting. You know what they are—and you know money can't buy them.

ACTION LIST

1. If you currently have a written budget and are feeling more and more guilty for not sticking to it, throw it into the trash. It's not worth the time and hassle to concentrate on "not spending."

    Date completed: _____

2. To get better educated, spend a few hours at the library and check out some interesting books on personal finance.

    Date completed: _____

CHAPTER 2

Goals: The Cornerstones of Saving

> No one ever accomplishes anything of consequence without a goal . . . Goal-setting is the strongest human force for self-motivation.
>
> —Paul Myer, lawyer and educator

Transforming Desire into Wealth

When I think about saving over the long term, I realize that doing it well is about being consistent with your habits. Disciplining yourself and making regular monthly payments to a savings or investment account is vital. The impetus for this commitment should be that you are doing the right thing for your future and your family's future. The mental aspect of saving is hard at first and often can make it difficult to feel good about all the money you are salting away. You could do many other things with that money to provide instant gratification. Unfortunately, for the most part our society teaches us how to part with it fast. But the long-term implications and payoffs make saving and investing a must for anyone.

The key reason people don't save is simply they don't know where or how to start. Napoleon Hill in his book *Think and Grow Rich* describes how important desire is when you try to obtain anything in life, especially more money. Hill spent years interviewing some of the most wealthy and powerful individuals in the world to learn their secrets. His book is not about how to become an instant millionaire by buying real estate or employing some other get-rich-quick scheme. The book is about doing what you enjoy and desire, and using that power to produce a life of abundance and prosperity for you and everyone you come in contact with.

If you want to enjoy a life of abundance and prosperity, you need to follow some simple guidelines, based on Hill's teachings, to help you achieve true financial independence. Do you want to be able to turn your money dreams into reality? You must follow definite steps to get there and not cut any corners in the process:

1. If you want something that involves money, you have to have in mind the exact amount it will cost. Whether your money goal is 10 months from now or 10 years, it doesn't matter. Having some flighty goal such as "I want lots of money to buy a sports car" just doesn't cut the mustard. Being definite will crystallize your dreams and desires in your mind.

2. Are you ready to give up something for your dreams and desires? You can't just wish something into being. You have to have the will to sacrifice a little for the reward you want. Describe in detail what it is you are willing to do to get your outcome.

3. When exactly do you want the results you are after? Be specific about the date you want to attain your goal or dream.

4. Now it's time to develop a game plan to get to your dreams. Write down the things you could do today to start on the road to achieving your goals. Don't worry if they don't seem perfect; you can always change your approach as the months go on. Just do something!

5. Review steps 1 through 4 and then write out a clear and precise "power statement" that incorporates all the main themes of those steps. Make it as specific as possible and don't worry about how long or short it is. Here's a great guideline to determine if it's powerful enough: It should send chills up your spine! If it doesn't, start over. The key point of this exercise is to step out of yourself and envision a life way beyond what you are used to.

6. Everyday, you need to read this statement out loud until you know it by heart. If you do this for just one month, you will have programmed your mind to know that you deserve what you desire and you will automatically do what it takes to make your dreams reality.

What is the most important component to make this formula for success work? I think it's about having the desire to succeed. If you want something badly enough, you will do what it takes to get it. If it means staying at work another hour every day, or starting a part-time business, you will do it. The formula just helps to make your desires more vivid and real. Remember that everything ever accomplished in this world started from a single thought in someone's mind. The mind is a powerful tool, so use your brains to help change your destiny. Destiny will then take over and change your life forever. As Napoleon Hill says, "Whatever the mind of man can conceive and believe, it can achieve."

I am living proof this formula works. And I still practice the steps every day. Let me point out this formula for success works with just about anything you want or desire in life. I sat down and wrote out specific goals and dreams for my future. Specific goals for 1, 3, 5, 10, and 20 years, such as when I wanted to build a dream house . . . how much I wanted in the bank . . . what kind of car I would drive . . . and what trips I would take, etc. The results were phenomenal. Not only have I reached the majority of my goals, but I went further than ever imagined. I live in a nicer home, drive a better car, travel more, and enjoy a much more pleasant lifestyle than I could have ever conceived. All this—simply because I truly desired my outcomes.

Of course, when I sat down and wrote out dreams and desires and tacked them up all over the apartment, I thought they were completely off the wall, so to speak. What I learned is that it is best to set your standards high because in the long run, your standards give you the opportunity to expand your vision of the future. All I did was put some excellent principles to the test, and they paid off.

I can't emphasize enough how important it is to use this formula for whatever you desire in your life. Use your own variations if you want, but stay within the general framework. I think you will find tremendous power in this formula that can positively affect your lifestyle. Without a doubt, the first step in developing a game plan for financial success is to focus on setting powerful goals.

Have You Ever Set Goals?

I was very distraught when I took an unscientific poll of friends and relatives to find out whether they set financial goals. They *all* told me they had a vague idea of how much money they wanted in the future. "Can you get a little more specific?" I said. "Well, I want to be a millionaire at some point, or at least be rich," one responded. What does that mean? Simply saying you want to be a millionaire only tells me you have some dreams that will never become reality. Why? In order to achieve financial independence, you must have specific, written, and identifiable goals.

It is vital that you make a list of things you want to accomplish in your life that involve money so you can focus on those things every day. If you don't write down these goals, your money will slip away when you go through the day-to-day financial grind. You just end up spending the money you had planned to save. You *must* write down specific goals with set time periods for the next year, 3 years, 5 years, 10 years, and 20 years. Write down exactly what the goals are and put dollar figures on them. For instance, "I want a new 2,300-square-foot white colonial house in three years." What will it take to get this? $10,000 or perhaps $20,000 in the bank for a down payment? "I want to send Johnny to Dartmouth College in 10 years." This goal might cost $100,000. Use this method to document all your financial goals and dreams.

The Rule of 72

The Rule of 72 is an easy way to figure out how long it will take to get the money for a specific goal. How long does it take to double your money in an investment? The answer is many years if you're only getting 4% at the local bank. Hopefully, you can manage a little better in other investments. You simply divide the number 72 by your expected return on your dollars, and the result is the number of years it would take to double your money if all the interest is reinvested and compounding.

For example, let's say you invested $5,000 in a mutual fund, and you expect a 10% return over the next several years. You divide 72 by 10, which yields 7.2 years. So after 7.2 years you should have $10,000.

Use this simple formula to calculate how much money you could have in the future. Go ahead, dream big. No one's watching.

After you have a list, tack it up on the refrigerator, on the bathroom mirror, and at your office. Make a smaller version of the list and put it in your purse or wallet so you see it every time you spend money. Repeat your goals to yourself in the morning and in the evening. If your dreams are in front of you all the time, you will be inspired to do whatever it takes to reach them. Believe me, the way you can achieve your dreams is evident once you are totally inspired.

Don't worry if your goals seem way beyond your means; dream about them anyway. You never know how or when your financial situation may change for the better.

Use these guidelines when you're outlining your goals:

1. Set your financial goals so you can work toward accomplishing important tasks with a clear, definable objective in mind.

2. Determine what's really important in your life and see how those things relate to your financial situation.

4. Recognize that financial goals are not set in stone; be flexible along your journey.

5. Always write down your financial goals and put them someplace where you'll see them often during the day.

6. Write down obstacles that stand in the way of your goals as well as the means that make them obtainable.

7. A good financial goal should always be easily defined and specific.

8. Find a great way to reward yourself when your financial goal is reached. Be creative and make that reward non-financial if possible.

By setting goals properly, you can make it easier to achieve them.

Fast-Start Goal-Setting

To help you get started right away, I have put together a goals worksheet, which appears later in this section. I have already given you the formula, but my experience is that most people do not follow up on great ideas unless they are made easier. This worksheet should make your goal-setting easier.

Money planning is a process designed to help you accomplish your goals. The nature of your goals and the way you meet them is of critical importance in your planning process. The process of money planning is on-going. Be prepared to review your goals every six months or so.

To review, ask yourself these important questions:

1. Where am I now financially?

2. Where do I want to be in the future?

3. How am I going to get there?

Keep these questions in mind as you set your goals and remember these pointers to help you along:

- Be specific and set target dates.

- Quantify your goals. Use specific numbers.

- Visualize your goals. Picture yourself having already attained the goal to strengthen your resolve to succeed.

Example:

Wrong: I want to live comfortably when I retire.

Better: I want to retire in 15 years at age 60 and live in a luxury condominium in Phoenix, Arizona. My monthly net income will be $7,000.

Now that goal is powerful! When you word your goals in this manner, you can easily measure your success objectively on a monthly or annual basis.

Now that you have an idea of how to formulate money goals, take the time to complete the following exercise. If you need more space, use a separate sheet of paper or any blank pages in the book. *Do it now!*

Goal-Setting Worksheet

Short-term goals (write down specific 1-, 3-, and 5-year goals):

(Example: Pay off Chevy loan in 21 months and buy my next car with cash.)

Goal	*Date*
Pay off car loan	in 21 months
_____	_____
_____	_____
_____	_____
_____	_____
_____	_____
_____	_____

Long-term goals (write down specific 10-, 15-, and 20-year goals):

(Example: Retire in 20 years at the age of 65. I will own a home worth $200,000 overlooking a lake and fish whenever I want.)

Goal	*Date*
Retire at 65 and own $200,000 lake home	20 years
_____	_____
_____	_____
_____	_____
_____	_____
_____	_____

continued

After you have listed your key goals, list the steps that will help you achieve the short- and long-term goals you listed in the preceding steps. (Example: Start a monthly savings plan.)

1. _____   _____
2. _____   _____
3. _____   _____
4. _____   _____
5. _____   _____
6. _____   _____

List three obstacles that may impede the attainment of the short- and long-term goals you listed. Remember not to focus on these, though. You will write these down just so you are honest with yourself. (Example: Excessive monthly credit card debt.)

1. _____   _____
2. _____   _____
3. _____   _____

After you finish this exercise, photocopy these pages and tack them up in places where you can see them often. Goal-setting is important because it makes you and your family examine values and then clarify them in writing. This practice enables you to plan ways to use available resources to reach your goals.

Finally, goal-setting puts you in charge and enables you to gain control of your money and your life. Do your goal-setting, then we can move on to the next chapter, which helps you understand exactly how to get to those goals fast.

ACTION LIST:

1. Spend some time thinking about what you really want out of life and how your finances fit into the picture. If you are married, involve your spouse so you can plan and dream together. If you have children, there is no reason not to involve them in the process also.

2. Fill out the goal-setting worksheet completely. Be clear, concise, and specific about the goals for your financial future.

    Date completed: _____

3. Copy the goal-setting pages and place them in highly visible areas around the house and at work.

    Date completed: _____

4. Read Napoleon Hill's book "Think and Grow Rich" as soon as possible.

    Date completed: _____

CHAPTER 3

How to Become a Green-Blooded Saver

"Rich People plan for three generations . . . poor people plan for Saturday night."

—Gloria Steinem

There's really no secret to becoming financially independent. It's not being at the right place at the right time, inheriting money, or possessing the financial wisdom of the ages. The simple rule is to develop a game plan for success and be persistent in executing the plan. Successful saving is not much different from playing football. Before a winning team walks onto the field, the coach has reviewed the plan of attack the team will use to beat the other team. The players start the game with the plan in mind and make adjustments to it as the game progresses. The team that wins is usually the one that has best executed its plan and made the right adjustments at the right times. When you're saving, you're playing against yourself rather than another team. Unfortunately, you're often your own worst opponent.

Don't think that you need to become a complete cheapskate to accomplish all your financial goals and dreams. On the contrary, becoming a $ensible $aver doesn't require you to drastically change your lifestyle. I'm realistic about the temptations in this "buy now, pay later" country, and I know many people need to have a few of the modern luxuries even though they may be living paycheck to paycheck. If I advocated some strict slash-and-cut saving plan that deprived you of all fun and reward, you would probably take this book and toss it in the trash. At the very least, you would not implement a darn thing I teach you. *The $ensible $aver* is just that: sensible. You need to establish a realistic plan to obtain all your dreams and desires, a plan that gives you some freedom in the process. I followed this plan, and you can, too.

The Power of Compound Interest

Most people don't realize that they will be a millionaire in their life-time. It's true. If you have an average annual household income of only $30,000 for 40 years, you will make about $1.2 million over the years. Pretty incredible, isn't it? Obviously, what's most impor-tant is not how much you make, but what you keep.

I suggest you begin saving a least 10% of your gross income as soon as possible. This amount may seem like a lot at first, but when you begin to save, you will find more ways to free up greater amounts. I save about 25% to 30% of my gross income on a rather modest salary. Of course, I didn't start off saving this much. It takes time and patience to get to this point. Even if you cannot manage 10%, the smallest amount of money saved systematically over a period of years will grow astoundingly using the power of compound interest. Einstein was once asked what he felt was the most incredible force of nature in the universe. He said it was compound interest, and he was not joking. He was astounded at the capability of one dollar to grow exponentially upon itself to eventually produce another dollar. I suppose, using Einstein's logic, that just as the "force" was to Luke Skywalker in the movie *Star Wars*, the "power" of compound interest can be to your savings.

You need only three things to use compound interest to your advantage: time, a little money, and some discipline. Every one of us has time on our side (some people more than others). If you use just a few of the money-saving strategies outlined in the book, I guarantee you can find an extra dollar or two to begin your jour-ney. Finally, with your sights set on a goal, you will develop the discipline needed to save.

I used to think interest was simple. If you put $1,000 in the bank and received 5% annually, you would have $1,050 at the end of the year. Then, if you received 10% interest the next year, you would receive double the $50, or $100. Wrong! Actually, the second year you would receive $105 because the 10% rate is calculated from the total of $1,050 you had after the first year. This process is called *compound interest* because new money keeps growing exponentially on top of the old money. The following table shows you the "power."

One-Time $1,000 Lump Sum Investment

Interest	20 Years	30 Years	40 Years
5%	$2,653	$4,321	$7,039
10%	$6,727	$17,449	$45,259
12%	$9,646	$29,959	$93,050

If you look closely, time and interest rate have a stronger impact on the money accumulated than the amount invested.

Do you think you can wait a while before you start saving? Think again. Let's say you wanted to invest $1,000 per year at an annual rate of 10%. The following table analyzes this scenario.

$1,000-Per-Year Investment at 10% Interest

Start Saving	Total at Age 65	Cost to Wait
Age 25	$487,852	———
Age 30	$299,127	$188,725
Age 35	$181,943	$305,909
Age 40	$109,182	$378,670

Finally, assume that you save $2,000 a year and invest it annually in a retirement plan, as the next table shows.

$2,000-Per-Year Investment in Retirement Plan*

Interest	20 years	30 years	40 years
8%	$100,845	$246,692	$561,562
10%	$128,005	$363,887	$975,704
12%	$163,397	$542,585	$1,720,285

* For illustration purposes, all figures are calculated assuming a tax-free investment.

If these examples don't inspire you, I don't know what will. Nothing can stop the power of compound interest except your unwillingness to become financially independent. So use the power to your advantage. Start putting money aside today!

How Much Should You Save?

You can do so much for yourself and your family by getting in the habit of salting away money every month. Even a modest amount saved today can make a big difference tomorrow as you can see by the preceding examples. If you want to reach your dreams and goals, you better start now.

How much you should save every month depends on a number of factors including your age, assets, income, expenses, and your goals. Saving is much easier when you have some concrete outcome in mind. Begin saving today for individual goals that are short-term and long-term. Put most of your energy into figuring out the next five years. Then decide how you can allocate your current savings to meet these goals. Consider goals such as buying a new home or car, retirement, and in a broader sense, complete financial freedom—as you define it.

In my opinion, as I wrote earlier, the average person should save about 10% of his or her pre-tax income yearly up to the age of 35. As you get older, the percentages should go up to about 15% at age 45 and 30% at age 55. These figures may seem high, but if you really want financial freedom, you need to salt away as much as possible.

Fill out the income/expenses worksheet later in this chapter to see how your savings stack up to the percentages discussed. If you fall short, try to figure out ways to free up more money for your future goals.

A good strategy to help you increase savings in the future is to sock away any bonuses and a percentage of pay raises every year. If enough years pass, just this money alone can compound tremendously. If you didn't expect this money anyway, you might as well earmark it for savings. Try setting even more money aside by implementing the tips and strategies included in Part II of *The $ensible $aver*. Often, you can put more money in your pocket by saving on things you are already buying than by clamoring for that $1,000 pay raise at work. Use as many of my tricks as you possibly can.

Many different factors may enter into your ability to start saving more, but the simple fact is if you are not at least somewhere around the percentages stated earlier, you will be falling short of where you should be in several years. If you want to ensure a great economic future for yourself and your family, you had better make the hard choices now and stop putting them off.

The "Bill Myself" Method

Pay yourself first. You have probably heard this advice before, and you will hear it again. The phrase means you must set aside money for personal savings before you pay anyone else—even the landlord or mortgage company. If you can pay yourself only $10 a paycheck, do it! I'm talking about starting good habits today that pave the road for success tomorrow.

The simplest way to find out how much you can set aside for savings is to use a method I developed called "Bill Myself." It is a simple and effective way to set aside money, and it doesn't demand much time or energy. Use this method religiously, and you will sock away hundreds, even thousands, of dollars every year.

To start, jog your memory for a half hour or so. Write down all the items you spend money on and the total of what you pay out during the month (see the worksheet later in this chapter). If you have no clue as to what you spend, go to your checkbook and review the last couple of months. This is the easiest way to find the specifics. After you have basic figures, review them and see if you are buying frivolous items that you could easily cut from the list.

After you have zeroed in on your spending, subtract it from your monthly income. The result is what you can save every month. If the figure is negative, go back and recheck your expenses and see if there are more unnecessary items you know you can do without.

Go to the local office supply store and get a booklet of generic invoices for yourself. Nothing fancy—the $1.98 variety does just fine. On the 20th of each month, write out an invoice to yourself for the savings amount left over from the preceding exercise. In the "from" section on the invoice, write the name of the bank or financial institution where you will be sending the money for your investment. You can also write in the "items" section exactly what account the money goes to. Be creative. Put this invoice in an envelope and mail it to yourself so it arrives with the rest of the bills around the first of the month. Before you pay any bills, pay this bill first, because it is by far the most important. If you prefer, divide the figure in half and write an invoice to yourself twice a month before each pay period. This method may work better because you don't need to plunk down all of the amount in one payment.

Of course you don't need to go to the trouble of mailing the invoice to yourself, but I have found that sending the invoice is another commitment to the process of saving. It is actually fun to get at least one exciting bill in the mail a month!

A good start is to put this money in a bank savings account. If you prefer a higher return, a money market mutual fund is a good choice. Let this money build to at least three months total income for any emergencies that may crop up. After that, you can start putting the money into other investments.

The reason I call my plan "Bill Myself" is obvious, but the reasons for its success may not be as clear. By sending money to your personal savings plan before paying any other bills, you are forced to live within what is left for the month. This method makes saving easy and automatic. If the money is not available to begin with, you are not tempted to spend it. In my opinion, this is the best way to save because the emphasis is on *saving* money rather than on *not spending*. The worse thing you can do is haphazardly spend money during the month with no idea of how you are spending it. With my method, money is always left over at the end of the month. The "Bill Myself" method eliminates worrying over having enough to pay yourself. At the first of the month you have already taken care of the most important financial event, sending money away for your future.

As you start saving month after month, and the money begins to compound in your savings account, you will be motivated to find new ways to free up more money to save. Saving can be fun and very rewarding. Check your plan every six months or so to make sure you are staying on track.

The $ensible $aver's Budget-Buster

I have provided you with a simple worksheet that helps you easily find out what your income and expenses are. The framework of this form follows the guidelines of the "Bill Myself" method. You may feel as if you are making some kind of budget, but remember that you are not going to be following this form day by day. Your objective here is to get a monthly savings figure to be your guide for the next several months. You take all your income and subtract expenses to come up with a number that is comfortable for you to save every month. The best way to get an accurate monthly figure is to average out variable expenses and incomes from the last year.

I urge you to take about 45 minutes to dig up the financial information you need to complete this worksheet and do your best to stick with the saving commitment you come up with. Make sure that you are giving yourself enough leeway with your expenses. Don't strap yourself so much that you end up having to dip into your savings account if you fall short at the end of the month.

Monthly Income

Salary
(include take-home pay for you and your spouse) _____

Self-Employment and Part-Time Income _____

Investment Income _____

Social Security _____

Veteran's Benefits _____

Pension _____

Misc. _____

Other _____

Total Monthly Income: _____

Monthly Expenses

Fixed Expenses

Mortgage/Rent _____

    Primary Residence _____

    Secondary Residence _____

Car Payments _____

    Auto #1 _____

    Auto #2 _____

    Auto #3 _____

---

continued

Insurance   _____
    Auto   _____
    Health   _____
    Home (if not included in mortgage)   _____
    Life   _____
    Disability   _____
Loans   _____
    Student   _____
    Personal   _____
    Business   _____
    Home Equity   _____
Alimony/Child Support   _____
Child Care   _____
Club/Association Dues   _____
Investment/Savings Plans   _____
Misc.   _____
Other   _____
Other   _____

Total Monthly Fixed Expenses: _____

Variable Expenses   _____
Auto Care   _____
Cable TV   _____
Car Phone   _____
Cleaning/Maintenance
(cleaning help, lawn service, etc.)   _____
Clothes/Accessories   _____
Credit Cards   _____
    Card #1   _____
    Card #2   _____
    Card #3   _____

continued

Charitable Donations   _____

Dry Cleaning   _____

Electricity   _____

Entertainment   _____

     Movies   _____

     Dining Out   _____

     Travel   _____

     Other   _____

Food   _____

Gifts   _____

Medical   _____

Natural Gas/Heating Oil   _____

Personal Care   _____

Pet Care/Supplies   _____

Sports/Hobbies/Lessons   _____

Subscriptions   _____

Telephone   _____

Transportation   _____

     Gas   _____

     Bus/Train   _____

     Tolls/Parking   _____

Water/Sewage/Trash   _____

Misc.   _____

Other   _____

Other   _____

Total Monthly Variable Expenses: _____

Total Expenses: _____

Total Monthly Income: _____

- Total Monthly Expenses: _____

= Total Monthly Savings Amount: _____

The monthly savings amount you come up with should be the amount of money you put into your favorite investment vehicle at the beginning of each month. If you have calculated properly, you should be able to live within the remaining expensed amounts. You should tap the monthly savings money only in case of an emergency or for a specified goal that you and your family agreed to in advance. If your monthly savings amount is negative, you need to do some work. Go back and see where you can cut out needless items from your expenses. This step may be difficult, but you will never get on the road to financial independence unless you make these hard choices. Again, review this worksheet every six months and update any figures or add any cost savings that are appropriate.

How to Break Your Spending Habits

The way to keep yourself from spending too much is the same way you get yourself to lose weight. Don't be discouraged by this statement because you may be thinking it's hard enough to lose even a few pounds. Saving takes discipline, and you need to break your spending habits down into bite-size portions so they're easy to handle.

Most people try to lose weight on crash diets. "Okay, tomorrow I'm going to stop eating so much," they say. Tomorrow rolls around and you eat a piece of toast for breakfast, skip lunch, and by dinner you're ready to stuff the refrigerator in your month just like yesterday. While you're chowing down, you think to yourself, "I can't do this diet thing. It's too hard. I'm a worthless chocaholic." This is exactly the opposite of what you should be thinking to produce lasting change.

The concept is the same with spending. If you try to change all your financial habits in one day, you're setting yourself up for failure. If you try to go cold turkey, denying yourself every opportunity to spend all at once, you will fall flat on your face. What's worse is that doing this type of spending freeze several times can make spending while saving seem like an impossible task. Just like preparing for the Olympics takes a tremendous amount of practice and time to build up to the big event, you need to take time to build up to your financial goals and dreams.

I have found that the easiest way to make more money is to learn how to spend smarter. You need to ease into less spending by looking at alternative ways to shop and save. Don't just stop spending. Keep spending but do it differently. I never buy anything over $50 without first checking at least one or two other similar products and stores. I have saved thousands of dollars using this method. Be willing to take a little time to research what you are buying, and don't just buy the first product that comes along.

My philosophy is that for every product you buy, another product exists that is less expensive and often better. Think of it this way: Most people normally see only one type of a certain product before they buy, but most of the time many more manufacturers of the same product exist throughout the country. Is it smart to buy the first item you see? No! Ease into taking control of your spending by doing more investigating. Many times you find that the more you look into products and services, the more you think about whether you really need it. You may end up deciding not to make the purchase at all.

Take the time to find things on sale. A sale is always going on somewhere. Look in the local newspapers and call stores in the yellow pages. If you save $20 or $30, it's worth the effort. You don't need to necessarily go cold turkey on the spending if you can save yourself a few bucks on sale items. But don't use a sale as a license to spend. This trap is common. Don't buy everything in sight thinking it's okay to spend your next paycheck because this or that was on sale.

The next step is to begin looking at what you are buying. Retrace your spending over the last several months and look at the things you have purchased. Have the purchases enhanced your life significantly? I'm willing to bet that many things have already been used up or discarded in a closet or your attic. You may be already sick of them. Smart shoppers can look back and see only items they really needed, not just wanted. In the meantime, these people put several hundred dollars in the bank for the big things in the future that they *really* need and want.

When you start looking into what you are buying and how you are spending, you will find that spending more wisely becomes easier. Overspending results from impulsively purchasing without checking the facts. Every time I think about making a purchase, Joe Friday comes into my head: "Just the facts, ma'am." I'm reminded immediately to think about whether I truly need this thing, and if I do, have I checked out other stores or similar products?

ACTION LIST

1. Complete the "budget-buster" worksheet in this chapter and commit to salting away your calculated savings amount every month. This figure should be at least 10% of your monthly gross pay.

   Date completed: _____

2. Next time you go shopping and need an item that is over $50, look at competitors' products of similar quality in the same store. Also, it may be worth it to go to another store to save an extra $10 to $20.

   Date completed: _____

PART II

Tips and Strategies to Save a Bundle

CHAPTER 4

Credit Control Basics

> *A banker is a fellow who lends you his umbrella when the sun is shining and wants it back the minute it rains.*
>
> —Mark Twain

The Seduction of America

Credit can be like a bad drug. It provides instant gratification when you use it. If you take too much, it can make you incoherent and cause you to do crazy things. Only later do you realize that you paid a tremendous price.

Getting credit today is easy. Just check the mailbox for your pre-approved Visa card. Walk into a car dealership with suspect credit, plop down a few hundred dollars, and the dealership "will work it out."

This chapter explains how you can control debt. You may find some conflicting advice, which I provided on purpose. As the saying goes, "one man's trash is another man's treasure." I have included several different ways to control debt, many of which can stand alone or work in conjunction with other strategies. You can choose the method, or methods, that work best for your situation.

I'm qualified to talk about this subject because I've been there. Chances are, you have, too. Almost all Americans have had problems handling debt by the time they reach age 40. Who hasn't experienced a rush of temptation when you realize that something you want badly is obtainable simply by putting a plastic card through the machine or by signing a piece of paper?

The reality is that employees of banks and finance companies across the country are being pressured by their superiors to loan, loan, loan. Why? Loaning money is a very lucrative business. A loan officer once told me that the best product he had ever sold in his sales career was money. If you had a million dollars and the opportunity to loan it out at a guaranteed 10% to 21% interest rate, wouldn't you do it? Add in all the extra money that will accrue in fees over the course of the loans, and you can see why loaning money is such an appealing business.

The problem is that debt can be a never-ending cycle for most people. At the end of last year, Americans had almost $300 billion in credit card debt alone. This figure represents about $2,000 per American taxpayer just on credit cards! Many of these people started with $200 balances on their cards, but instead of paying this amount, they just made the minimum payments and kept on chargin'. Some people even need to get a cash advance on the card to pay the minimum payment, which may approach $250 per month. Then when the credit limit is pushed to the ceiling, the consumer needs to decide whether to pay the credit card company or the mortgage company. When you hit this credit wall, something needs to give, and when one wall falls, the house comes tumbling down. It makes me sweat just thinking about it.

Why, with so much stress in our daily lives from work and home, do we insist on overextending ourselves? Home is where the heart is and where serenity is supposed to be. Can you think of anything more stressful than not being able to pay the mortgage, phone, or electric bill? Do you like getting overdue notices in the mail or receiving harassing calls from bill collectors late at night? Why do we inflict this punishment upon ourselves?

It's simple. We live in a get-it-now society. Like the alcoholic, we are addicted to getting it or else. The finance companies and banks get rich off this addiction. However, don't put all the blame on them. We have only ourselves to blame.

You can use credit in three ways:

1. To purchase perishables such as food, gas, and meals. These items are absolutely the worst things to buy with credit.

2. To purchase depreciable items that have only short-term value such as cars, clothes, furniture, and electronics. Because these purchases lose value fast, it's still not the best idea to buy them with credit.

3. To purchase appreciable assets such as a house or other investments. These items are really the best things to finance with credit.

Credit is just a game. The first rule is that you must take personal responsibility to keep your bills under control and pay them on time. If you don't play by this rule, you will pay the price and perish. It's no one's fault but yours if you can't play the game within the rules.

The important thing to remember about any purchase bought on credit or with loans is you don't own what you are buying until you have paid the debt. The lender owns it. Many former millionaires have learned this lesson the hard way. When you miss a couple of payments, the lender takes control and becomes your master.

Next time you nonchalantly pull out that American Express or Visa, or sign the loan papers on a new car or boat, ask yourself, "Is this debt going to add to my addiction or will it benefit my financial well being?" Don't be seduced any longer. All Americans need to wake up from the hypnotic spell we have placed ourselves under and start living within our means. On the count of three, you will awake. One . . . two . . . three.

Do You Have Too Much Debt?

Even if you don't have creditors calling you constantly to get money, you still may be close to getting squeezed by your debts. If your monthly payments on short-term and personal debts (car payments, credit cards, department store debts, student loans) exceed 20% of your net income after taxes, you may be in trouble. This amount does not include your mortgage, of course.

The average consumer has more than 7% of his or her take-home pay in personal debt. If your debts exceed this amount, you will need to make some changes so you can avoid nasty phone calls from bill collectors down the road.

If you are in over your head, vow to make all your payments no matter what. Review your expenses and try to free up as much income as you possibly can, and begin the debt pay-off strategy discussed later in this chapter. You would be smart to free up about 2% to 5% of your net income to start paying off your debts. Do not go too high with this figure or you could get into even more trouble.

Quit charging while you work on paying down the debts. More charges will make you feel as if you are spinning your wheels after several months. If you are in serious trouble, you may need to curtail all discretionary spending for a few years. That's right—no more new cars, trips, or stereo equipment for a while.

If you cannot make your payments on schedule, get in touch with your creditors and tell them what is happening. If creditors are familiar with your situation, they are much more likely to cut you some slack. The last thing to do is try to hide. If you do not return calls and try to avoid them, creditors will opt to take quicker action against you. Most creditors will work with you as much as they can rather than go through costly and time-consuming legal action, but this is only if you communicate honestly. Often, you can negotiate short-term relief based on how much you can pay each month.

Look at trying to lower the interest rates on your payments where possible. Investigate refinancing your mortgage if you have not already done so, or consolidate your high-interest credit cards onto a lower-rate card if you can find one. Many cards are offering introductory rates of 6% to 7% for a year to get you as a customer. Be careful, though. You need to read the fine print of the agreement before you just pick any card. If you consolidate onto a low-interest card, vow to pay it off within the allotted time.

If you can find a low-rate home equity loan, consolidate higher-interest loans into this one loan. You may also consider taking out a loan against your retirement plan at work. But use these strategies carefully because the fees or tax penalties can negate any savings you will realize. Paying off debt with another debt is a good tool only if you have changed your spending habits and have the discipline to not use your new freedom to charge more.

Seek dependable help if you feel overwhelmed by your debts. Contact the non-profit Consumer Credit Counseling Service (800-388-2227). Counselors can help you work with your creditors to design a reasonable payment plan that is within your means. The advantage to using CCCS is that you need to make only one payment a month to CCCS, which is responsible for making distributions to your creditors. CCCS charges only about $10 per month for this excellent service. If you are considering bankruptcy, the best thing to do is contact CCCS first.

How to Get Completely Out of Debt Fast

You may have heard or read that to be completely out of debt is impossible and stupid. The reasoning behind this statement is that if you were to pay off your mortgage, for instance, you would lose the only tax deduction you have left. Confused by this reasoning, I asked my accountant, "Why would I want to pay the huge interest on a mortgage only to save 20% to 30% of it on my taxes? Wouldn't it be better if I didn't have to pay any interest to begin with?" My accountant looked at me rather puzzled and said, "I have never thought of it that way, but I don't know many people who have their mortgage paid off, so that wouldn't apply."

That wouldn't apply? Does this mean the logic doesn't hold up? I don't think so. After 30 years with an average $100,000 mortgage on your home, you will have paid the bank a total of $300,000. You will have paid the bank $200,000 in interest over this time, twice what you paid for the house. Moreover, you are probably paying much more than this amount if you, like the average American, move into a different home every five to seven years. If so, then your monthly payments are about 95% to 98% interest in these first years, and you're getting practically no equity buildup in your home. Five to seven years later, you end up starting all over again. In essence, you are paying the bank a huge premium to use their money for only a few years. Mortgages are designed to be paid off over the term of the agreement, not rolled over into a new mortgage every few years. The bank is using the power of compound interest against you. Actually, when you procure any type of loan, you will always end up having the power of compound used interest against you.

You may be thinking it would be nice to pay off all your loans including your mortgage and have lots of money to save every month. Most people think this situation is possible only if they get an inheritance or win the lottery. Actually, paying off all your debt *is* possible if you follow some simple steps that will give you total financial control over your destiny. This is true financial freedom. Wouldn't it be incredible to not have to grovel to some banker to purchase a car or a house?

First, determine the amount of extra money you want to set aside to start paying off your bills. This money will start your debt payoff engine. The amount doesn't need to be much; $50 to $100 per month is a good starting point. This money will compound as the months go by, so don't think it is too small to make a difference. Try to make this amount about 10% of your total monthly debt payments, if you can. If your total payments on all debts is $1,000, then your initial amount is $100. Let me point out that the total of your bills obviously doesn't include your utilities, groceries, rent, etc. I'm talking about payments on money you owe to banks, the mortgage company, credit card companies, etc.

Make a pact with yourself to not get deeper in debt. Cut up and throw away all your credit cards. This step makes it much harder for you to charge and rack up more consumer debt. If you find that a credit card is necessary for emergencies or to travel, search for a bank that gives you a Visa or MasterCard debit card with your checking account. A debit card gives you the convenience of a charge card, but the money comes out of your account immediately, just like a check. You also can use an American Express card because you are required to pay off the bill each month. I prefer the debit card, though, because you usually have no annual fee. The important thing is to not give yourself the ability to instantly charge and add to your debt.

Gather all your debt bills together. Then write down each account's total balance and its corresponding monthly payment on the following Get Out of Debt Worksheet. For credit cards, write down double the minimum monthly payment as the total. This amount is usually only about 4% to 6% of your total balance, so don't think you can't afford to double this small payment. Now, rank the payments in order of your lowest payment to highest payment, with the lowest being number one, the next highest number two, etc. Determine a ranking for each bill and write down the rank next to the monthly payment figures. You will pay off your bills in this order. Most likely, you will be paying off charge cards first, consumer and car loans next, then your mortgage.

Don't worry about which accounts have the highest interest rate, because you're focusing on acceleration of debt payoffs. Because you're going to pay the debts fast, the amount of interest you pay is not as important as the speed in which you do it. You want to turn the power of compound interest in your favor as soon as possible, and you want to feel like you are accomplishing something when you start to pay off debt after debt.

The amount you have determined will be used to help start your plan is the extra amount you should now pay to bill number one every month until it is paid off. Of course you keep making your regular payments, too. You will most likely pay off a credit card bill in about six months instead of continuing the minimum monthly payments for years. After you pay off this debt, take the initial extra pay-off amount *plus* the amount you were paying to bill number one and apply it to bill number two. Of course you also continue to make the regular monthly payments on bill number two.

Continue this process for every bill in the order it is ranked. By the time you get to your car and mortgage payments, the extra amount you are applying will be huge, and you can pay off these debts fast.

In most cases, you should eliminate all your small consumer debt, including car loans, within the first 12 to 18 months of the plan. You will then have an extra payment to apply to your mortgage that may be equal or even greater than your normal mortgage payment. Wouldn't it be incredible to put all this money toward your mortgage principal every month?

Using this system, most people can become completely debt-free within five to seven years. This beats 30 years by a mile. Use the following worksheet to calculate how long it will take you to become debt-free.

Get Out of Debt Worksheet

Date: _____

Debt Account	Total Balance	Monthly Payment	Extra Monthly Pay-Off Amount	Pay-Off Date
_____	_____	_____	_____	_____
_____	_____	_____	_____	_____
_____	_____	_____	_____	_____
_____	_____	_____	_____	_____
_____	_____	_____	_____	_____
_____	_____	_____	_____	_____
_____	_____	_____	_____	_____
_____	_____	_____	_____	_____
_____	_____	_____	_____	_____
_____	_____	_____	_____	_____
_____	_____	_____	_____	_____

---

continues

_____	_____	_____	_____	_____
_____	_____	_____	_____	_____
_____	_____	_____	_____	_____
_____	_____	_____	_____	_____
_____	_____	_____	_____	_____
_____	_____	_____	_____	_____
_____	_____	_____	_____	_____
_____	_____	_____	_____	_____
_____	_____	_____	_____	_____
_____	_____	_____	_____	_____
_____	_____	_____	_____	_____
_____	_____	_____	_____	_____

Totals: _____ _____

The biggest advantage to this plan is not having to come up with a lot of extra money up front to pay off debts (or win the lottery to do it). The following commitments are the only ones you make:

- Stop adding to your debt.

- Apply a small amount of extra money to start paying down your debt.

- Live at the same overhead level you are now for however many years it takes to get completely out of debt.

I think these sacrifices are very small for the unbelievable rewards you can produce by eliminating all your debts and having 100% equity in your home. Then you can look forward to operating 100% on cash and becoming your own banker for the rest of your life.

Cash Is King

Pay cash whenever you can for consumer goods including clothes, groceries, dining out, movies, and miscellaneous products. You should have the cash in your wallet or the money in your checking account. The reason to pay cash for these items is because they don't make you any more money to help offset the finance charges. These items lose value. Resist the temptation to pull out that plastic unless you are absolutely certain you will pay it off when the next bill comes. Going into debt makes sense only for something like a new home or other investments. Debt on consumer goods can be the biggest detriment to your savings account.

Defer Nothing

Be cautious about advertisements promising deferred payments for six months, or no payments until next year. These offers may require that you put a huge amount of money down to "hold" the item, or they may include an outrageously high rate of interest—21%—if you do not pay off the loan within the allotted time. The offers sound great, but often you'll end up paying more for the item than if you had waited six months and paid for it in cash.

Car Loan Blues

If you can afford to, buy a new or used car from your savings instead of taking out a car loan. The interest you pay for a car loan generally is more than you can get in a good savings account. You need to look at the after-tax rate you earn on your savings to get a precise look at the difference. If you are in the 31% bracket, subtract 31% from your investment earnings. For example, if you are averaging 10% in a mutual fund, you will technically have only 6.9% once Uncle Sam gets his hands on his share. When you look at the situation this way, you find that purchasing your automobile with cash is much more attractive. If you don't have the cash, look into taking out a home equity loan. You can deduct interest on this type of loan, which effectively reduces the amount you need to pay the bank.

Credit Card Basics

When I think of credit cards, visions of scissors dance in my head. How nice it would be to lose the temptation of the pliable plastic that works so well running through those machines.

But, as the $ensible $aver, I must sometimes deal with the shocking realities of life. At Acme car rental you may hear, "Sir, you need a credit card to rent this car." At the department store, "Sir, do you have a second form of identification, preferably a credit card?" Ordering over the phone, "Sir, you can put these plane tickets on hold only with a valid credit card."

I have tried the toss-the-credit-card technique and it gave me only grief. Having a card can be vital as an important convenience and in emergencies. I know credit cards are important because sometimes relatives call wanting to borrow mine—it is often the only way they can buy something.

I have found that it's okay to have a credit card, but these pointers can help in controlling the urge to splurge on the plastic:

- Use only one credit card, preferably a Visa or MasterCard because they are more widely accepted. Avoid the status cards like American Express and Diners Club. The only advantage to these cards is you must pay them off at the end of the month. These companies charge a fee, however, for having the "privilege" of flashing the card in front of friends or business associates.

- Use your credit card only when absolutely necessary such as renting a car, purchasing plane tickets, and in emergencies.

- Pay off your entire balance when you receive a bill.

- If you are carrying a balance, consolidate all your credit debt onto a single low-interest card to make it easy to stay on top of the debt.

- Take out a home equity loan to consolidate many other loans as well as credit cards. The advantage is that all your interest is tax deductible.

- Never make minimum payments on the balance. Always at least double the payments.

- As mentioned earlier, get a MasterCard or Visa debit card that is tied to your checking account. If your bank doesn't offer this service, find one that does. This is becoming a very popular service at banks around the country.

To find out about the best interest rates on cards throughout the country, contact Bankcard Holders of America, 524 Branch Dr., Salem, VA 24153, (540) 389–5445.

One Call Can Cut Your Rate

You can cut your credit card debts significantly with just one telephone call. If you are carrying high balances on several cards that have high interest rates, call a bank that offers a lower introductory rate than what you are currently paying. Explain that you would like to transfer the balances on your other cards if you can get the best rate. I know of instances where rates were cut by 6% to 7%. Ask whether the bank can also waive transfer fees. If the bank refuses, try another card issuer.

This strategy also works well if you are happy with your current bank or credit card company but feel the interest rate is a little too high. Simply call the bank or institution that issued the card and ask them to lower your interest rate. Sounds too good to be true? Well, it works. Tell them you think your rate is too high and would like it lowered to a more acceptable rate because you have been such a good customer.

You decide what's acceptable. If you're an aggressive negotiator, you can sometimes get as much as four percent chopped off your rate. If the bank balks at your request, say that you will transfer your balance to another card. Because so much competition exists among credit card issuers, a card issuer usually would much rather give you a lower rate than lose you as a customer.

The Black Hole

Low interest rate credit cards can end up costing you much more if they lack the standard 25-day grace period for new purchases that most cards have. The last thing you want is a credit card that immediately starts assessing interest when you buy something. This fee can far outweigh any interest rate reductions you may be getting for a period of time. Even if you pay off your balance at the end of the month, you are still paying interest month after month. If you are thinking about changing to a new card, read the fine print of the contract well. Look for cards with no annual fee and a 25-day grace period on new purchases.

Also, some credit card companies can really cheat you. For example, suppose that you owe $1,000 on a card. You pay $950 on the day the payment is due. Your finance charge should be calculated on the remaining $50, right? Wrong. Many cards calculate the interest based on the average daily balance, which in this case was $1,000. To avoid this kind of charge, always pay off your balance every month by the due date.

Never take cash advances on your card. Some cards charge a higher interest rate on advances plus an extra fee. Effective yields can be as much as 30% on this cash!

If you see a new card advertised with an interest rate of less than 10%, chances are that rate lasts only for a short period of time. A rate that is 6% for six months and then jumps to 20% afterward is a sucker's deal unless you are absolutely certain you will pay off your balance at the end of six months and religiously pay the monthly balance from then on. If the difference between a card's introductory rate and its long-term rate is more than 7%, look elsewhere.

How to Make 18% on Your Money . . . Guaranteed

Sound incredible? Well, it really isn't when you consider how to do it. Do you have any credit cards or high-interest loans that are not paid off? Take care of these balances immediately, especially those loans or credit cards with 15% or 18% interest. In essence, you will be getting these high rates of return on your money. Use my debt pay-off strategy outlined earlier in this chapter to give yourself a running start.

I recommend that you take a close look at your outstanding debt and try to balance paying it off with a good savings plan. A good rule of thumb is if you have loans that are at 9% interest or greater, double up your monthly payments and get them paid off. You may want to be even more aggressive by using my debt pay-off strategy. Having this debt linger on for years only prolongs your financial insecurity.

Some people make an argument for having no debts except their home. I think living by this strategy is excellent because if you ever get into financial difficulties, you don't have thousands of dollars of debt to exacerbate the problem. I feel there is a good possibility our country will experience some tough economic times ahead, so having as little debt as possible will be an advantage. Being debt-free is a kind of *insurance*. If we do have major economic problems, excess debt may be a burden that will bring many people to their knees.

My grandparents lived most of their lives buying everything, even their homes, with money they had in the bank. They lived through the depression and understood how bad times could get. Through the years they have always said, "If you don't have the money to pay for it, don't buy it." You may not get to the point where they were for some time, but when you are there, you can have true financial security and not be dependent on a bank or finance company for your well-being.

This philosophy is not for everyone, and above all, I'm realistic about the personal finance habits of many Americans. But working toward a goal of at least having your high-interest debt paid off is a positive step in the right direction.

Credit Repair Made Easy

Many new ads push credit repair services and lawyers who charge between $200 and $2,000 to "clean up your credit" by saying they can remove all the negative items on your personal credit report.

If you hear these lines, run for cover, because this task is not possible. Negative, but accurate, information stays on your report for 4 to 7 years and as long as 10 years with a bankruptcy. No one can change this documentation. However, you can clean up bad credit by lowering your debt load and replacing the bad credit with good credit. If you can show that you have had great credit for two to three years and that the other blemishes were just mistakes, a creditor may see you have gotten back on track and give you the benefit of the doubt.

If you get a credit report that contains wrong information, simply write a letter to the agency stating your disputed items and ask the agency to remove the items from your report. The agency will investigate the items and send you a letter of the results. They are required to perform this duty by law. Some credit reporting agencies have dispute forms that come with your report because mistakes are common.

If you are turned down for a loan because of an obvious mistake on your credit report, take matters into your own hands. Checking the accuracy of your report once a year makes sense. A good percentage of credit reports contain errors.

Many credit bureaus charge you for a copy of your report, but legislation in Congress has made it easier for consumers. You can obtain a free copy of your report once a year from TRW. All other credit bureaus give you a free report if you are turned down for credit. To get your free report from TRW, write to TRW Customer Service, P.O. Box 2350, Chatsworth, CA 91313. You need to include the following information:

Full name

Current address and all addresses in last five years

Social Security number

Date of birth

Spouse's name

Copy of your driver's license

Check the report for errors, and contact the bureau if you see any discrepancies.

If you need to improve your credit or completely start from scratch, a secured credit card is a great place to start. With this type of card, you deposit money in a bank savings account, and the card issuer uses the money as collateral. If you put in $250, for example, you can charge up to $250. Once you have an excellent payment record, you improve your credit. You can contact the Bankcard Holders of America (address listed earlier in chapter) to get information on the best secured cards in the country.

Remember that you have as much power to improve your credit as anyone else. Don't pay anyone to do the impossible. Save your money by "cleaning up" your own credit.

The Pitfalls of Bankruptcy

As dreadful as it seems, especially to the $ensible $aver, more and more people are looking at bankruptcy as a way to escape financial troubles. The number of individuals as well as businesses filing for bankruptcy protection is growing to alarming levels. In 1985, 298,000 individuals filed for bankruptcy in the United States. By 1995, that number exploded to over one million! That's a 70% increase in just 10 years.

People file for many reasons—spending with no regard for the future, an investment goes sour, job loss, massive medical expenses not covered by insurance, etc. Bankruptcy is beginning to lose the stigma it once had because so many more bankruptcies occur today.

The types of bankruptcy for which individuals usually file are Chapter 13 or Chapter 7. Chapter 13 consists of developing a plan to repay debts over a period of three to five years during which the court keeps a watchful eye. Sometimes the repayment is less than the debt's original value. Under Chapter 13 filing, a household budget is formed, and creditors receive what is left after basic expenditures. You may be able to keep part or all of your assets.

On the other hand, Chapter 7 filing is straight bankruptcy that liquidates most of your assets and frees you of all debts. You can keep the equity in your home, car, household goods, and jewelry. Some states have more liberal bankruptcy laws than what the federal government requires, so filing under the state's guidelines may be beneficial. You can receive a discharge from your debts under bankruptcy protection once every six years.

To file, you can buy a bankruptcy kit and petition the federal court by yourself, but it is best to see a qualified bankruptcy lawyer, especially if you have a complicated situation. Listen to your lawyer closely to determine whether he or she is explaining all your options or is unduly pushing you toward bankruptcy filing.

Consider filing only in dire circumstances. I have received letters from people with only $4,000 to $5,000 of debt who feel filing for bankruptcy is the only way to alleviate the enormous weight on their shoulders. These individuals are often depressed for other reasons such as the loss of a job, but they believe the debt is causing the depression. Typically what they need is credit counseling, debt restructuring, and reassurance that things will get better. Bankruptcy definitely does not promote self-esteem, and it leaves a black mark on your credit record for up to 10 years. Declaring bankruptcy makes obtaining or refinancing a mortgage very difficult.

If you believe your debt load is insurmountable or you think it will restrict you financially and emotionally for many years, bankruptcy may have its place. Wiping the slate clean and starting over can help emotionally. A few firms extend credit to bankrupt people, operating under the theory that a further bankruptcy is not possible for seven more years. Life is not over after bankruptcy, but it is more difficult.

If you are seriously considering bankruptcy, first explore all other possible options. Contact the Consumer Credit Counseling Service in your area. This service can help you devise a plan to repay your debts without filing for bankruptcy. Counselors help you set a realistic budget, and they negotiate with the creditors, on your behalf, to lower your monthly payments. You pay a very small amount because CCCS is paid by the creditors.

If you are determined to declare bankruptcy, let the dust settle for a few months. Given time, your finances can change dramatically.

ACTION LIST

1. If your credit load is more than you can bear and you are having to run from your creditors, consider cutting up your credit cards and not adding to your debt load. Don't let credit control your life.

    Date completed: _____

2. Is your goal to get completely out of debt so you can live a life 100% with cash? If so, complete the "Get Out of Debt Worksheet" and begin applying an extra monthly amount toward those debts.

    Date completed: _____

3. If you must have a credit card, consider a debit card issued by a local bank. This option gives you the advantages of a credit card but the money comes directly out of your checking account.

    Date completed: _____

4. Order a free copy of your credit report from TRW to check up on your credit standing. TRW Customer Service, P.O. Box 2350, Chatsworth, CA 91313.

    Date completed: _____

5. If your current situation has you considering bankruptcy, contact the nearest local office of the Consumer Credit Counseling Service (800-388-2227).

    Date completed: _____

CHAPTER 5

Slash Your Shopping Receipts

> *A bargain is something you have to find a use for once you have bought it.*
>
> —Ben Franklin

The average American spends approximately $16,000 per year buying groceries, clothes, jewelry, appliances, and other disposable items. Although many of these costs may seem unavoidable because, after all, we all need to eat and wear clothes, many are frivolous wastes of our money. The key is realizing what you really need and what you don't need.

Whether you're in a grocery store or a department store, you can use tricks and techniques to stretch your dollars and pay as little as possible. All it takes is a little extra time, effort, and knowledge about the right ways to shop.

The Great Coupon Myth

One way manufacturers try to convince consumers to buy their products in grocery stores is with coupons. Because most manufacturers build the cost of coupons into their products, you are paying too much if you don't use a coupon. No doubt coupons can save you money, but some major drawbacks can make saving coupons a pain for the average shopper.

First, no one likes to spend endless hours clipping and organizing their coupons so they can use the ones they need at the store. Secondly, the lure of coupons makes it easy to buy products you don't want or don't regularly use. Often, you can end up spending more than necessary when you use coupons.

You can find coupons in magazines, newspapers, on products, and in the mail. Coupon exchanges located in stores or the local library can be a good source to find coupons, but searching through the endless piles and checking expiration dates still is tedious. The simplest form of exchanging is with friends and relatives. Remember to use only the coupons you really need.

If you use coupons, find a local store that has double or triple coupon days. These offers can really save you a bundle. The store simply doubles or triples the coupon's value and deducts it from your bill. You often cannot use the discounts on products like alcohol and tobacco. Some stores also limit the allowable deduction per coupon to one dollar. Even so, you still can easily save $10 to $15 per grocery store visit if you take advantage of these special days.

Above all, don't be swayed by the marketing value of a coupon. Use your own criteria for judging the products' quality and value. I'm a fan of generic or store brands and urge you to consider this option before you automatically use a coupon on a name-brand product. Many times the generic product is a better buy than the name-brand product, even if you buy the name-brand item with a coupon. You must look at coupons as a part of your savings plan.

These additional tips may help you:

- Shop only at stores accepting competitors' coupons, which are often in Wednesday's newspaper.

- Clip coupons only for items you would normally buy.

- Shop at stores that offer double or triple coupon values. You may even be able to get items for free.

- Shop in the morning when you're alert and the shelves are well stocked.

1-800 Bonanza

Most products have toll-free phone numbers on the packages. Call the companies of products you use the most and ask for coupon samples. Many companies are more than happy to send you coupons. If you use these coupons often, you can save a bunch.

Good Ol' Generics

When shopping at grocery stores, pay special attention to generic and store-brand items. Most people have different preferences about what they may or may not like in these off-brands. Here are just a few things you can buy at savings of 50% or more that are almost always the same quality as the name brands: flour, sugar, trash bags, tin foil, ammonia, bleach, salt, pepper, vinegar, light bulbs, and baking soda. Keep your eyes peeled for others.

Convenient Rip-Offs

Why do convenience stores have great deals on coffee and drinks? Because they know most people who buy these beverages usually purchase one or two other items at 50% to 100% more than regular grocery stores charge. Don't ever purchase anything at a convenience store other than coffee and soft drinks or you might as well take dollar bills and burn them one by one.

Space Your Shopping

Limit your major grocery shopping to once every two weeks. This practice limits your impulse-buying tendencies and also saves a lot of time. You can pick up items such as milk, eggs, and perishable meats when you need them. Just remember, don't buy them at a convenience store.

Units Are the Thing

When grocery shopping, pay special attention to unit pricing, which lets you compare different products according to how the units—in ounces, servings, or pounds—are priced. Many times you may assume that a larger size is a better buy. The only way you can tell is by checking the unit price. If you just take a few minutes to calculate this measure, you can save quite a bit.

Bulky Purchase

Buying in bulk is a great way to save money and needless trips to the grocery store. The problem is that you are spending lots of money up front to realize the savings. Make sure you will use all the product, and don't buy tremendous amounts of bulk items at one time. To calculate the savings with bulk purchases, use the unit formula described in the preceding section.

Scanner Troubles

A recent study of supermarkets showed that they charged incorrect prices on over 10% of items! Overcharges were much more likely to occur than undercharges on electronic scanner systems. Some grocery stores were found to be deliberately tampering with prices in the computer systems, but most errors came from pricing over-sights. The government is now investigating.

To avoid being overcharged, you need to do a little more work at the grocery store. When you shop, have a detailed list of things you put in the cart, and mark down the price next to each item. Put a star next to all sale items. When you go to the checkout counter, watch the scanner read-out carefully. You may catch some oversights immediately. After the clerk finishes ringing up the groceries, take the receipt and compare it to your list. Don't do this at the check-out counter. Instead, step aside for the next person so you are in no one's way. Make sure you do your comparison at the store so you can show the clerk any errors immediately and also save your-self the hassle of having to make another trip back to the store.

If you regularly find problems at the store where you shop, look for a more efficient store. Contact your state's attorney general if you think deliberate fraud may be involved.

Shopping Pangs

Avoid shopping for groceries on an empty stomach, or you'll probably spend 10% to 15% more. Make a list and stick to it. This practice curbs any impulse-buying desires you may have.

The Butcher's Right

Have you ever noticed chicken is a lot cheaper when you buy it whole rather than cut up? You pay extra for the butcher's knife. Sometimes the difference is tremendous and makes you wonder how much these people get paid. I know butchers aren't getting rich, so the store must be making all the profit. Always buy a whole chicken at the grocery store and cut it up yourself. The same applies to buying meat already cut. Cutting a steak into chunks doesn't take much. Also, be careful about buying meat with the fat cut away. You pay top dollar for this service when you can very easily cut the fat away from a less expensive piece of meat.

The Breakfast Cereal Fiasco

Whenever I go to the grocery store, I'm stunned by how much cereal costs. Apparently Congress is also dismayed. Congressional hearings have investigated allegations that price fixing and gouging have occurred in this industry for some time. The Justice Department is also conducting an investigation into these allegations.

If you ask me, no investigation needs to done. It's pretty obvious that the manufacturers are gouging us when you see cereals priced at $4.99. What's in these boxes—gold nugget flakes? However, don't hold your breath waiting for the government's investigation to conclude. We may not see any changes in prices for years. In the meantime, here are some alternatives to buying name-brand cereals:

- Look more closely at store-brand or generic cereals. Sure, some may not taste the hottest, but if you experiment, you can usually find one or two varieties that aren't too bad. In recent taste test studies, many generic Cheerios beat out the name-brand stuff. The generics also save you a bundle.

- Look at buying name brands in bulk. Many stores and grocery warehouses offer certain brands in bulk quantity, which takes your unit costs down considerably. Also, you can buy some better-quality store brands in plastic bags rather than the expensive boxes. I do this and save between $1 and $2 per box.

- Try alternatives to packaged and ready-to-eat cereal. Some good options are oatmeal and Malt-o-Meal.

- Better yet, make other breakfast meals that don't include cereal. Bacon and eggs, pancakes, toast, fruit, and juices are still great American standbys. Is it necessary to have Tony the Tiger at the breakfast table?

Seasoned Greetings

At the grocery store, you pay 15% to 60% more for products that include added sugar, seasonings, and other extras that you can easily mix together yourself at a lower cost. Pre-sweetened cereals are probably the best example. You typically pay about 50% more for a box of frosted corn flakes compared to regular corn flakes. The only difference in quality is the sugar coating. You are better off if you buy the regular corn flakes and pour a cup of sugar into each bowl. Yuck, can you believe we eat this stuff? Also, beware of frozen vegetables. A bag that includes its own sauce or seasoning costs about 60% more than the same size bag without the sauce. Plain versions also have less fat.

Nifty Thrifty

Do you cringe when you think of going into a thrift store or Goodwill shop? If you do, you may be losing out on great shopping opportunities. Not too long ago, I dropped into the local thrift store to see if I could find anything good. Most of the stuff seemed like junk to me, but I was able to find two pairs of almost-new khaki pants for only $3. With $15 worth of alterations, I saved about $60 off the retail cost of similar pants. One of my newsletter subscribers told me that he does all his suit shopping at thrift stores. Often, you can find a fashionable outfit that just needs a little tailoring and dry cleaning to make it like new.

Designers Put in Place

A designer label doesn't always mean better quality. Although a designer probably designed and made the dress or suit you buy, many other items carrying the designer's name are almost always made by another manufacturer. Shoes, coats, hats, purses, and bathing suits are commonly "farmed out" to other companies that may not have the same quality standards of the designer. Designer labels are always accompanied with a 15% to 20% increase over ordinary garments. Sometimes the item is worth it, but more often you are just paying for the name. Scrutinize these items just as you would any other purchase. Don't rely simply on the name.

El Largo

When you plan a budget for clothes, be realistic in your tendency to gain or lose weight. A wardrobe of classic clothing is useful only if it fits properly. Changing sizes, whether you gain or lose weight, means buying new clothes. Although you may have great intentions, don't purchase clothes two sizes too small hoping to lose weight to fit into them. I don't think any studies have been done on laboratory mice in this same predicament, but my feeling is you will have lots of unused clothes around if you buy smaller sizes.

Discount Shopping

You don't always need to pay full price for an item if you see an imperfection. Do not hesitate to ask for a discount or demand an item that is not flawed. If you shop at any local stores frequently, get to know the managers and ask them to tell you when they are having a sale. Also, get on the store mailing list if there is one. In small stores, it's not uncommon for the owner to give you a discount if you frequent the store or to give you a special item free. Many owners do what they can to keep a loyal customer. All you need is one simple formula: just ask!

Also, a good idea is to shop at outlet stores in your area to save significantly. It is probably worth it to drive a few hours if you have to. Outlet malls are springing up all over the country and Americans are flocking to them in droves. The reason is simple: The quality is great and the prices are cheap. I recently went on a shopping excursion to a mall about 90 miles from my home and saved about $90. I figure a dollar a mile is well worth the effort.

Save Bucks on Books

Next time you think about buying a book, you may want to keep the following pointers in mind:

- Look in the Yellow Pages for chain discount book stores in your area. These stores usually discount most books and also have deep discount racks throughout the store. You can save as much as 30% if you shop selectively. Some of these stores offer a discount card that provides even greater discounts if you purchase a certain amount of merchandise from the store over a selected period of time.

- Check local wholesale clubs that sell in high volume. Their prices are excellent on recently published and bestseller books.

- Consider joining a book club if you read a lot. You get a certain number of books for $1 or $2 plus shipping when you join the club. Then you receive new releases every month or so. You can save $50 or more per year if you tend to read one book or more per month. Make sure you are dealing with a reputable company, and by all means read the fine print at the bottom of the contract before signing. You also must be prepared to send a notification to the company if you don't want the latest month's selection. Some clubs just send you the book, and if you don't like it, you need to send the whole package back. What a hassle. Again, read the tiny print at the bottom of your information sheet. Also, keep track of what you really spend with these clubs to see if you are getting the savings you expect.

- Two great places to get bargains on books are garage sales and used book stores. I'm amazed at the number of quality books available at garage sales. People want to get rid of the clutter on their bookshelves. Ironically, you may find many recently published books at these sales, which gives you an idea of how quickly the $30 books get tossed out of the house. A good negotiator should be able to pick up most books for less than a buck.

- Talk with friends and relatives who are avid readers. Work out some kind of exchange where you can read their books and they can read yours. This is a great way to read lots of books.

- The greatest way to save on books is to visit your local library. The library has about every book under the sun, and you don't pay a dime—unless you bring the books back late. I think that libraries are the most under-used resource that Americans have at their disposal. We are so used to *buying* things in this country that we think there's nothing worth a darn available for free. Visit your local library and tell me if that's true.

College Book Beats

If you have children in college, books can take a big bite out of college savings. Check out the campus bookstore for used textbooks that are sold on consignment when other students have completed the courses. Your child also may be able to resell those books to the book store when the course is finished. Find out the name of the books needed and make some calls to used bookstores located near the college. You can usually find several popular books and may save as much as $100.

The Day After

You can save some big bucks by purchasing holiday items the day after the big day. For instance, you generally can buy Christmas lights and ornaments for 50%-75% off after December 25. Even if you buy too much tinsel for next year, you'll use it sooner or later. Candy drops dramatically after Halloween and Easter. Wine and liquor costs are excellent right after New Year's Eve.

Gift Relief

Throughout the year, it's a good idea to think about buying gifts when you shop. If you see items on sale that would make great gifts later in the year, buy them and store them in a special gift closet at home. It's good to have Christmas, birthday, and anniversary gifts on hand so you don't have to rush to the store a day or two before the big event. If you see the right things on sale, you can save a tremendous amount of money instead of having to pay last-minute prices. If secrecy is a problem (those nosy kids), store the gifts in a lockable chest or at a friend's house for safekeeping.

Make Your Pet Cheaper

Buy pet food and supplies at a discount pet supply store. Many cities now have pet supply warehouses where you can save as much as 40% on selected products. If Fifi or Fido gets the best in food, then these stores can save you a lot because they mark down high-quality products tremendously. Last time I went to the local wholesaler, I saved 35% off what I was paying at our vet for the same cat food. These discounters also carry a wide range of pet care products below retail. Check your local Yellow Pages for the discount pet store closest to you.

Dial and Save

Why settle for the best deal in town when you can be shopping all over the country just by picking up the phone? You can save tremendous amounts of money by shopping with the various discount mail-order companies throughout the country. You can save on appliances, furniture, household gadgets, and electronics just by calling these companies and asking for catalogs. You also can find items like clothes, art supplies, and sporting goods.

How do you save on big-ticket items? The average consumer doesn't know about the great services offered by price-quote companies because they don't advertise. But these companies are eager to please and can save you a bundle. Make sure you know exactly what you want, including manufacturer, model number, and other descriptive details.

Here's a sampling of some of the best price-quote companies carrying different products:

- *Furniture*—Cedar Rock Furniture carries all major brands of furniture at up to 50% off retail. Address: Box 515, Hudson, NC 28638. (704) 396-2361.

- *Appliances*—EBA Wholesale offers dozens of products from more than 50 name-brand manufacturers including Admiral, KitchenAid, Panasonic, Westinghouse, and GE at savings of up to 60%. Address: 2361 Nostrand Ave., Brooklyn, NY 11210. (718) 252-3400.

- *Automobiles*—Nationwide Auto Brokers can send you a form ($9.95) showing you all the optional equipment available on the car of your choice and then arrange local delivery with your dealer. You automatically save between $500 and $4,000 just by letting Nationwide negotiate a dealer-to-dealer price break that eliminates the need for a commission. Address: 17517 W. 10 Mole Rd., Southfield, MI 48075. (800) 521-7257.

- *Computers*—CMO offers name-brand computers like IBM, Apple, and Hewlett-Packard as well as other systems and software for about 40% off retail. Address: 2400 Reach Rd., Williamsport, PA 11701. (800) 233-8950.

- *Fitness equipment*—Better Health and Fitness can get you what you need to complete a home gym for up to 25% off retail. Address: 5302 New Utrecht Ave., Brooklyn, NY 11219. (718) 436-4801.

To locate a price-quote firm in your area, turn to the item you are looking for in the Yellow Pages. You usually can find listings for national companies that sell the product. The discount firms tip you off with ads that have phrases such as "wholesale prices" or "all name-brands at discount prices." Not all products will have discount firms' listings, but you should find a few.

If you are looking to buy smaller items, there are hundreds and hundreds of fabulous catalogs you'll never know about unless you scour newspapers and magazines to find their ads. You also may hear about the catalogs through word of mouth.

These catalogs offer you the opportunity to buy your favorite products at discounts, and you don't need to waste time trekking through busy shopping malls. You can find catalogs for just about anything from the mundane to the exotic. Here are some less-known but great catalogs for the picky consumer:

- *Art supplies*—Cheap Joe's Art Stuff sells paint, canvas, mat cutters, and art books at 30% less than retail. Address: 300A Industrial Park Rd., Boone, NC 28607. (800) 227-2788.

- *Fragrances*—Essential Products Company can save you up to 90% of what the real perfume would cost—if you don't mind wearing good-quality imitations of designer fragrances. Address: 90 Water St., New York, NY 10005. (212) 344-4288.

- *Bed and bath*—Harris Levy can help you save as much as 50% on Wamsutta, J.P. Stevens, Springmaid, and other manufacturers. Address: 278 Grand St., New York, NY 10002. (212) 226-3102.

- *Quilts and Collectibles*—You can save as much as 30% on antique quilts when you buy from Quilts Unlimited. Address: 440-A Duke of Gloucester St., Williamsburg, VA 23185. (804) 253-8700.

- *Boating supplies*—Goldberg's Marine Distributors can save you up to 60% on boating equipment and nautical clothing. The company delivers your shipment in three to five days. Address: 201 Meadow Rd., Edison, NJ 08818. (800) BOATING.

- *General merchandise*—If you are looking for a great general catalog that has all sorts of items from toasters to toys, browse through Damark International. You can receive substantial savings on a variety of name-brand products; in some cases prices are as much as 70% off retail. Address: 7401 Winnetka Ave. N., Minneapolis, MN 55440. (800) 827-6767.

Whether you call a price-quote company or a mail-order company, be sure you ask about the return policy. Sometimes you pay a substantial charge for returns. Use a credit card to further protect yourself, and make sure you keep a record of your order and all receipts. Frequently, people forget about their order; unfortunately, without documentation, you can do little at that point.

Computer Savvy

More and more Americans are jumping on the bandwagon and buying personal computers. PCs can be powerful tools to help organize your life, but you need to know about some pitfalls.

It's very important that you seriously evaluate your specific needs before you plunk down two grand or more for a good system. I recommend that you have at least three or four great uses in mind before you make the plunge. You may need the computer for word processing, budgeting, spreadsheet capabilities, or perhaps a database. If you own a business, as I do, you may find a personal computer to be invaluable. If you want one just to play games, then I strongly advise you buy a Nintendo. The graphics are better and you will save hundreds of dollars.

The easiest way to find out how a computer can help you is to spend some time looking over software. Most metropolitan areas have stores that sell software exclusively. If you have some basic uses in mind, ask a store clerk to guide you to the best software programs. By choosing software first, you get an idea of the power and speed capabilities you need in a computer. Many computers are sold with software bundles that may have just the software you want.

Two main types of computers exist: IBM (or IBM compatibles) and Macintosh. I have had both computers and think the decision is a real toss-up. If you don't know a thing about DOS (the operating system for the IBMs), then I suggest you go with a Macintosh. Macs are much more user-friendly, and you don't need to go through the difficult process of learning the DOS operating system. One thing about IBM, though, is that it's the standard for most businesses, which means you have many more software choices. Getting an IBM or compatible may be a better idea if you run a business. Also, the Windows software program makes operating your DOS-based sytem much simpler.

Be very careful not to purchase a model that is old or out of date unless you have just one or two simple applications in mind. Computer technology is changing so fast that you may be left in the dust. Statistics show the life of new computer technology lasts only about a year and a half before it's surpassed. When the technology changes, so does all the software, and you don't want to find yourself unable to run your favorite software packages. Consider buying the latest computer if you want to keep up for several years.

You can buy an adequate computer system for around $1,600 at a local electronics discount store. You probably can get decent speed with all the latest multimedia capabilities. Stay away from laptops if you are making your first computer purchase. Laptops have very small keyboards, are much more expensive, and lack upgrade options. It's best to get a desktop computer and then later add a laptop if you can't survive without one.

Speed is all-important in a computer because it determines how well your software programs run. If you purchase an IBM or compatible, I suggest that you buy a minimum 486 microprocessor (the chip that runs the whole system) running at 50MHz (megahertz). A 586, or Pentium chip, is much faster but costs more. Again, your decision rests on the tasks for which you are planning to use the computer. If you will use huge programs and many business applications, then a Pentium may be your best choice. If you use the computer for word processing, budgeting, and things at home, a 486 may be just fine. Make sure your computer has at least 8M (megabytes) of RAM (random access memory) and a large hard drive to store all your applications. Your hard drive should be about twice the size you need to begin with.

If you're looking for something inexpensive, I suggest that you check the local classifieds to find a good used computer. You may find a computer that is only a year or two old and has all the fetures you want. You can save about 50% or more by going this route. Make sure you check out the computer thoroughly before you buy. Have the owner hook up the computer, then spend an hour or so checking all the applications and printing out documents.

Buying a computer is a big investment, and you should definitely comparison-shop before making your purchase. If you are thinking about buying a new computer or accessories, check the stores in your area. Computers have come down in price considerably the last few years, and all the retailers are out to beat the competition. I recently saw two different store ads in the same paper that were offering a similar computer package, but there was a $200 price difference. I'm sure the more expensive retailer was very frustrated that its ad happened to run on the same day as the other ad. You might consider picking up a computer magazine and calling numbers to receive a few computer discounter catalogs. Many of these warehouse discounters can offer savings of 20% off what other retailers charge. Consider also looking into computer resellers in your area; insist on a warranty if you go this route.

Check Floor Models

You can save by buying appliances, electronics, or furniture off the floor. If you can live with the merchandise having some nicks and dings, you can save as much as 50%. Actually, you can use these flaws to your advantage to negotiate the best deal possible. I've had several brand-new items delivered in the past that had scratches and dings right out of the box. What's the difference?

Should I Get an Extended Warranty?

Beware of extended warranties. For most modern appliances and electronics, manufacturers' warranties are all consumers really need. Besides, extended warranties are over-priced and are rarely used. Often, when something does go wrong with the appliance after the manufacturer's warranty runs out, you have no idea where you put the extended warranty paperwork and without the appropriate documentation the warranty may be void. Extended warranties may make sense, however, for big ticket items that have a tendency to break such as gas range ovens, large-screen TVs, and camcorders. Make sure you read the fine print in any warranty before you pay for it. Cost and coverage vary widely.

Barter Is Better

Consider bartering services with friends and neighbors, especially when money is tight. Several times I have exchanged subscriptions to my newsletter for different services. Sometimes you don't come out even, but if you barter often, the results seem to work out well for everyone. In addition, you build stronger business relationships with individuals using bartering. Centuries ago, bartering was the only way man did business in the world. Money has simply replaced what I feel was once a much more personal way to trade. So the next time you are thinking about buying something to make your life easier, consider exchanging a service you provide for someone else's services. You may both come out ahead in the long run.

If you don't run a business, you can also barter with friends and relatives. For example, if you are a good cook and your neighbor is a good gardener, you may want to exchange a meal or two for the planting of some tomato plants. You can be very creative with this because anything you don't particularly like to do can usually be bartered out.

Also, consider pooling your money with friends and relatives to buy bulk items at wholesale stores or butcher shops. If you have a good relationship with a grocer at a local store, you can usually negotiate price breaks if you purchase large quantities. You can also pool your money with friends or relatives to purchase a boat, RV, or a vacation home.

Engagement of Terror

You can get taken when you shop for an engagement or wedding ring if you aren't hip about how to bargain. The best thing to do is visit as many dealers as possible so you can educate yourself. Keep in mind that jewelry is one of the highest mark-up items in the retail industry. Many people hear an ad on the radio and say, "That's the place for me to buy." Then they get suckered into a deal that is really not right for them. One way to save quite a bit is to buy your ring at a diamond wholesaler. You should also think about buying a loose stone at a designer show and having it mounted in the setting of your choice. Finally, never spend more than you can afford; you can always upgrade in several years when you have the money.

Shave and a Haircut

Are you fed up with the high price of getting a permanent or a haircut? By going to a local cosmetology school, you can save as much as 60% off retail. Most schools don't require appointments and usually have managers checking on the work of the students. The one thing you may sacrifice is time. Getting your hair done at schools takes longer because the students check and recheck their work. After going to a cosmetology school well over 50 times, I can honestly say I had only one poor haircut. That number is pretty good considering I've been to "professionals" and can remember several times when I walked out of the shop with a buzz cut. I have saved a bundle by giving the students practice. Check your local Yellow Pages for a school near you.

Beware of Buying Clubs

Buying clubs are becoming popular throughout the country. I have found that most clubs do not offer a tremendous amount of benefits, even though the benefits are touted in the sales literature. Quite often, clubs mail slick brochures and fancy letters that make it look like you get the world by joining. After you sign up, however, you may find that the discounts offered are no different than what you could have gotten yourself by doing some homework. The companies selling the memberships usually pay nothing to give you these benefits because the vendors in the program pay to get customers. So anything they charge you is generally pure profit, over and above advertising and administration expenses. If you are totally convinced a buying club is a good deal, I wouldn't pay more than $25 annually.

Home Shopping Come-Ons

Too many people are being taken in by the lure of home-shopping channels. Although many of the products sold are of good quality and may be priced right, the companies that run these networks rely heavily on bored, alienated consumers who sometimes shouldn't be spending *any* money. Tempted by powerful marketing, consumers often buy more than they need or can afford because they become fixated with the personalities selling the product on the tube. Many addicted consumers ask for the same order-taker when they call because they view that person as a good friend. If you feel you may be caught in this situation or you know someone who is, turn the tube off and evaluate the problem. You may need to pursue other activities to take the place of home shopping.

ACTION LIST

1. When shopping at the grocery store, pay special attention to generic products and buy in bulk when you can. Scour the Wednesday and Sunday papers for coupons, but use coupons only for products you would normally buy. Don't buy name-brand breakfast cereal unless you feel you must.

   Date completed: _____

2. Visit a local thrift store in your neighborhood and check out the bargains. You may find several things of value.

   Date completed: _____

3. If you are considering a major purchase, call one of the discount mail-order companies mentioned in this chapter.

   Date completed: _____

4. If you have never tried bartering before, experiment by putting together a simple bartering situation between yourself and a relative or a business associate. Always try to make it a win-win proposition.

   Date completed: _____

CHAPTER 6

Automobile Savvy

> *Guys, just remember . . . If you make a lot of money and go out and buy stuff, it's just gonna break . . . . Things just don't mean happiness.*
>
> —Ross Perot

Many of the letters I receive from my newsletter subscribers ask for steps on how to save on buying and maintaining cars. It's no wonder, because the average American goes through about 15 cars in his or her lifetime. What amazes me is how people get so wrapped up in saving pennies on clothes and groceries, then go out and blow all their savings on an overpriced car. Because the average car costs about $18,000, you can understand why car manufacturers are eager for you to buy the latest and greatest model. They are betting that if they put you in their car, you'll come back and buy several more cars from them in the years to come at equally outlandish prices.

Buying and maintaining the monstrosity in the driveway offers a great opportunity for you to save thousands of dollars—if you use some common sense in your choices. To have *car savvy* means to have the knowledge to beat the car sharks at their own game. Using this knowledge, you can save up to 30% on new cars and even more on a used car. You also can significantly reduce the cost of maintaining these wallet-draining transportation devices.

Buying a New Car

Although I advocate buying a used car for value, I know that a large percentage of the population still will buy a new car. There is something about the shiny finish that attracts even the best of savers. Maybe this fascination says something more about the slick advertising. We have definitely been well conditioned.

If you are dead set on a new car, make sure you plan to keep it for a long time. You need to negotiate the best deal possible and plan to drive the car until it dies to get full advantage of the premium you pay.

Should I Buy or Lease?

It's difficult to explain why leasing is advantageous for some people. If you listen to the car salesperson's pitch, you may wonder why you ever thought about buying. A lease sounds sooo good! You have no down payment, the payments are lower, and you can deduct the amount you pay. These are the "facts" the dealer gives you. Trying to read a lease agreement is like trying to decipher Egyptian hieroglyphics.

I'm going to dispel some of the myths associated with car leasing and give you some pointers so you don't get suckered when you decide to buy a new car.

- *Myth #1: Leases don't have down payments.* Wrong. What's the difference between putting $1,000 down on a car you are buying outright or coughing up $250 for a security deposit and $375 for the first and last month's payments on a lease? You tell me. Maybe the difference is that this amount is not called a *down payment*. It's obviously a much better deal for you if you buy outright and just ask to have the first month's payment deferred for two months. Most finance companies don't have a problem with this arrangement. If they do, find another financing source.

- *Myth #2: The payments are less on a lease.* You are paying for the difference between the price of the car now and the car's expected value in the future, usually in two to five years. In many cases, this future value figure can be trumped up or down depending on the resale value of a particular model. How does anyone really know what the car will be worth at that future time? Because you are not financing the entire sale amount of the car, you can understand why the lease payments are lower. Payments may be lower, but of course you don't have a car at the end of the payments unless you pay that residual value in a lump sum.

- *Myth #3: Leases are tax deductible.* You can deduct the lease payment only if you use the car for business purposes. Many a car salesperson has led an unsuspecting customer into this trap because most people associate leases with tax deductions. Never fall for this line.

- *Myth #4: You don't pay any interest when you lease a car.* When you ask about the interest rate (APR) on the lease, you're often told, "Leases don't really have rates—it's just how the lease is set up." Baloney! Leases have what is commonly called the *implicit percentage rate* or *yield*. Just ask for the yield if you get embroiled in heated negotiations. Dealers are required by law to quote you this rate. Most people get burned by paying way too much in interest. Some finance companies have been known to charge well over a 20% yield without the customers having any inkling of what is going on. State regulators are beginning to crack down on the hiding of this rate.

What is the real cost of the car? You must find out the real cost— the price you would pay for the car if you bought it rather than leased it. In the leasing biz, this price is called the *capitalized cost.* Ask the dealer to show you the capitalized cost in writing on the lease agreement. Walk away from the deal if the dealer refuses.

After you know the capitalized cost, follow these rules to get the best leasing deal if you're dead set on getting a lease:

1. Add any trade-in, factory rebates, and down payments. Subtract this number from the capitalization cost. This number is the *net cap cost.*

2. Subtract from the net cost the amount listed on the lease as *residual value* (what the car will be worth at the end of the lease).

3. Add the amount called the *lease charge.* This charge might include administrative fees, special insurance, and sales and use taxes.

4. Divide the amount in step 3 by the total months in the lease. This amount should be equal to your proposed monthly

payment. If the monthly payment is higher, you are being overcharged.

This formula may sound a little confusing, but the fact of the matter is that leases are confusing. If you are intent on leasing your next car, be prepared to dig into the fine print to get the best deal possible.

How can you negotiate the price of your car intelligently if you don't know the capitalized cost? If you have doubts about what you are really being charged, ask your local banker to tell you the yield rate and the capitalized cost on your lease. If the interest rate is over 11%, you better start asking some questions. Ask the salesperson for a copy of the documents and have your banker look them over. (As a matter of fact, I recommend this review with any lease arrangement.) Leases are extremely complex documents for average folks like you and me.

Remember, too, that leases generally require you to have the highest possible car insurance protection because the finance company wants to protect its investment. This insurance can cost hundreds over the lease term. Never buy credit life or disability insurance coverage because these policies are inflated by 50% over what you would pay for regular coverage. Also, decline extended warranties that will make the finance and insurance company richer and you poorer.

As you can probably tell, I'm not a big fan of car leases because you can be zapped in about 10 different ways. Leases are just too complex. Wait a minute, dealers, I'm not saying that good leases don't exist. From time to time I have seen some attractive deals, but very few. Buying is much smarter because the deal is simpler and you own the car when you are finished making payments. You also can get a better deal on the car when you buy it outright.

You may need to sacrifice a few extra dollars every month if you buy, but it will be well worth it when you own the car in the end. A lease situation is similar to buying a house as opposed to renting. If you rent a house for 30 years, you don't want to see that your neighbor is having a mortgage-burning party as you sit with not a penny in equity just because you wanted to save $100 a month.

Timing Your Auto Purchase

There are good times and bad times to buy a new car. The best time to buy is November when the new models start to come out. You can get last year's models, which are actually still the current year's, at a reduced cost. Also, buy during a prolonged period of dismal weather when showrooms are deserted. (Avoid buying in the early fall, when most people buy.) Another slow time for the dealers is at the end of the month when they are usually looking to meet quotas and move cars out of the dealership, regardless of cost. Always avoid buying a new model when it first comes out. That's when its market value is the greatest.

Negotiate Your Best Deal

The first place to start your car negotiating is at the library. I know it sounds crazy, but the library is where you should begin your research into the real cost of the car you want. Pick up a copy of *Consumers Digest* or *Consumer Reports*. These publications tell you exactly what that car costs the dealership. Armed with this knowledge, go into the dealership at the optimum time of the year/month and start negotiating. If you work hard enough and the dealership really wants to move the car, you can often swing a deal for less than the invoice cost. This approach works best at high-volume dealerships—you know, the ones with the goofy car dealer in the television ads running around in a funny hat. Don't worry, though, dealers still make money because the manufacturer pays them incentive bonuses for moving the car. Armed with the dealer's cost, you can negotiate confidently when they swear to you that the car cost them X dollars, and you know it's hundreds of dollars less. If you have to, pull out a copy of the cost listed in the magazines.

Borrowing Facts

If you can, try not to borrow money when you buy a new car. When you borrow, the car actually costs a lot more because of the tremendous amount of money you pay in interest over time. The more you borrow, the more you'll pay in interest, and if you borrow for a longer period of time, the bank charges a higher rate of interest.

If you can't avoid borrowing, opt for the shortest term of the loan you can manage. If you are a true *Sensible Saver* and are concerned about your payments, here are the ways to buy a new car—in order of best to worst:

- All cash
- Big down payment and short-term loan
- Smaller down payment and short-term loan
- Big down payment and long-term loan with high interest rate

Demo Deal

Consider buying a demonstration car from the local dealership. Quite often these cars are still in good shape and are virtually new. Insist on a new car warranty that protects you if the car turns out to be a lemon. Also, insist on an extended warranty if you purchase from the dealership.

You also may want to consider buying a car from a rental agency; look for one with the lowest mileage. Have an independent mechanic check out the car thoroughly before you buy so you know you aren't purchasing a car that has been abused.

Buying a Used Car

A common misconception is that if you buy a used car you are buying someone else's headaches. I think the qualifier to this statement should be "if you aren't smart," you will buy someone else's headaches. There are good used cars and bad used cars. The key is to make sure the car is mechanically and structurally sound before you buy.

Most new cars depreciate about 20% once the car leaves the dealership lot. Cars depreciate another 15% to 20% by the second year of ownership. This is roughly a 30% to 40% drop in value in just two years. Why not take advantage of this drop and buy your next car used? If you do some homework, you can find a well-maintained two-year-old car with an active life of 70,000 miles or more left; it may likely have some of the factory warranty remaining. If you buy a high-quality car like a Mercedes or BMW, you may be able to get another 100,000 to 150,000 miles out of the car plus several years left on a bumper-to-bumper warranty. Even though I am *The $ensible $aver*, I drive a high-quality car because I don't believe in settling for less. I bought a year-old Jaguar for below its wholesale value. I could drive it for a year or two and then sell it for close to what I paid for it. Great used car deals like this are out there. You just need to look hard and be a good negotiator.

Ten Things to Avoid When Buying a Used Car

1. Interior rust. Exterior rust is a sign of what's to come; interior rust is a sign of what is. Check between doors and seams and underneath the trunk. If rust eventually eats through the trunk, exhaust fumes can enter the car and cause health problems.

2. Fluid leaks of any kind. Stop and look for another car.

3. Brakes that don't operate smoothly.

4. A noisy engine or clicking noises. Listen for rattles, sputters, and squeaks.

5. Strong smoke that could mean major engine damage. Some exhaust smoke is normal; look for drastic smoking like billowing white or black smoke.

6. A strong, musty smell inside the car, which could mean the car was in some sort of flood or it has a leaky roof. Repairs will be costly.

7. A car that has been seriously wrecked.

8. Annoying rattles throughout the car. This could be a sign that it has structural problems. The rattles will only get worse as the years wear on.

9. A verbal agreement. Always get everything in writing.

10. Buying the car without having it inspected.

Never take the seller's word for the car's condition. Take it to a qualified mechanic for inspection. Pay a few extra dollars and confirm you are making a good decision by getting a detailed opinion from a mechanic. Even if the car is in good shape overall, you may be able to negotiate the price even lower if the mechanic finds other little problems.

Buy Direct from the Owner

You are usually better off buying your used car directly from the previous owner rather than a dealership. A dealer is likely to charge you about 20% for the "privilege" of buying off the fancy lot. The dealers are not always trying to sucker you, but they need to pay huge amounts of overhead in their businesses. They have to make as much as they can on the deal. Personal contact with the present owner usually allows you to get honest answers to your questions without high-pressure sales tactics. About the only downside to buying from an individual is you don't get a one-year warranty, which a dealer often provides. Therefore, make sure to have a mechanic inspect a car you buy from an individual, just as you would inspect a dealer's car. Even if you end up buying your dream used car from a dealership, insist on talking to the previous owner (most dealers will let you if they really want to sell the car and are not hiding anything) so you can find out if anything is seriously wrong with the car.

Sell Your Used Car Yourself

How would you like an extra $1,500 in cash the next time you decide to get rid of your old car? By using a few tricks and putting a little time and effort into fixing up your car, you can keep the cash you normally sacrifice when you trade your car to a dealer.

The first thing you must understand is that dealerships almost always give you a terrible price for your used car. Even if your car is in good shape, the dealer may give you hundreds or even thousands less for it because they need to make a tidy profit when reselling the car. If the dealer doesn't want to put the car on the lot, then it is sold at auction. On the average car, the dealership usually gives you $1,000 less than the auction price. This all spells a bad deal for you.

Car salesmen can use your trade-in as leverage to manipulate the deal. If you think the trade-in price is fair, the dealer generally tells you the car is great and is in demand. In reality, the dealer is relying on you not knowing your car's value to inflate the price of the new car. If you object to the trade-in price quoted, the dealer often tells you that your car is not worth very much and isn't in demand. Never trade in your used car!

How can you personally sell the old clunker for the maximum value?

First, you need to determine the true value of your used vehicle. Call your local banker and ask for the National Automobile Dealers Association (NADA) retail value of your automobile. The retail value is the price at which a used car lot might sell your vehicle. But don't expect to get this amount unless you are the world's greatest salesperson. You should settle for somewhere between the NADA trade-in value of the car and the NADA retail price. Remember that the trade-in price in the NADA book is not the arbitrary price that a dealership might place on your car. NADA lists the car's true trade-in value for loan purposes.

After you have determined your selling price, clean your car to perfection. Detail the inside, wax the finish, and clean the engine at a local pressure wash facility. If you don't want to clean the car yourself, or you just don't have the time, hire a service. For about $100, someone else can make your car look like new. You will recover the $100 several times over when you sell your car. In addition to cleaning, fix any minor mechanical or noticeable problems. The important thing is to get your car in shape so it makes a good first impression.

The next step is to advertise your vehicle. Advertise in the most popular local paper and also in a car shopper newspaper. Of course, weekends are the best time to advertise, but don't ignore special week-long advertising deals. Take a look at some current ads in the paper for ideas on what you should include in your ad. Something catchy always helps. Make sure you put your asking price in the ad to encourage only serious inquiries. Your asking price should be $300 to $500 more than you really want.

Consider setting up just one appointment for all the potential buyers to view the car. This arrangement adds perceived value to your car because all the viewers wonder why so many other people are looking at your car. Nothing sells a product faster than getting the buyer worried about whether he or she will "miss out." To avoid no-shows at your viewing, get potential buyers' names and addresses when they call so they feel they are obligated to show up.

Have a dollar figure in mind that is absolutely the lowest amount you will take for your car, and stick to it. When you're not wishy-washy about the price, the buyer is aware that you know what the car is worth. If the buyer quibbles at your price, take out a copy of the NADA book with the listing for your car. When the deal is done, accept only a cashier's check as form of payment. Never take a personal check.

Be as prepared as possible with paper work and details about signing over the title. The more you know about the rules and laws, the faster you can get the car sold.

Color Your Car Rich

The color you choose for your car when you purchase it can mean more money in your pocket when you resell. Red and beige are the safest colors because they have the best resale values. Medium and dark blues also sell well. Green cars are the worst sellers, followed by white, yellow, and metallic colors. The reason is simple: most people aren't as used to seeing these colors on the road as readily as red, blue, and beige. You may not consciously realize it, but the color of your car is of utmost importance if you want to get the most money when you get rid of it.

Do You *Need* a Car?

If you live in a big city, owning a car can be an outrageous expense. Unless you need the car to get to work, consider not owning one and just renting when you absolutely need to have one. If you rent a car for only two or three days a month, you come out way ahead of what you would pay for a car loan, gas, insurance, parking, and maintenance. You often can get great rental car discounts if you tend to use a car on weekends only. Use public transportation or ride your bike or moped to work. Any of these options can save you as much as $6,000 per year.

Rental Car Insurance Dilemma

Should you buy that optional rental car insurance from the rental car company? If you want to make the rental car company rich, go ahead. Some companies charge double the daily cost of the car if you buy all their optional coverage. Most credit cards have insurance coverage for rental cars if you pay with your card. Check with your card issuer to see if you qualify. If not, check with your car insurer to see if you have extra rental car coverage. If you don't, you usually can purchase coverage for a nominal fee.

Pocketing Slick Bucks on Oil Changes

If you hire someone to change your oil, go to a franchised oil-change center rather than the dealership where you bought your car. Change your oil every 4,000 miles, not every 2,000 to 3,000 miles as recommended by many new car dealers. Dealers want you to bring your car in for costly "maintenance checkups" that quite often turn into overpriced oil changes anyway. Take your car to the local oil-change center and save up to 50% on routine service. Also, these centers often do several other checks on your car and don't charge more for this service. You often can get coupons from your local paper or through the mail to save even more. If you really want to save some money, have your mechanic show you how to change the oil yourself.

Cool Move

When you're driving at speeds above 50 miles per hour and need fresh air, turn on the air conditioner and don't roll down the windows. It does cost to run the air conditioner, but today's cars are designed to run best when they can maximize airflow and reduce drag on the car. If you roll down any windows, the wind resistance significantly reduces fuel economy and will cost you more than just running the air-conditioning.

You Pay a Premium for Premium

It is a myth that premium gasoline makes your car run better. In fact, recent studies show that premium gasoline may even hamper the running of many cars. Why? Many premium gasolines are refined through different processes that alter their basic chemical make-ups. Most cars have a problem utilizing these specialized mixtures because they are heavier. Premium gas can result in bad combustion, vehicle hesitation, higher emissions, and even stalls. Always check your owner's manual and use the recommended gasoline for your car. Most manuals recommend regular-unleaded. Don't get fooled by ads claiming that more costly premiums "clean" your engine. The best way to keep your engine clean is to change the oil regularly.

Pressured Savings

The days of the full-service gas station are over, so it's up to you to check the pressure in your car tires regularly. Why? When your tire pressure is low, you lose 2% in gas mileage efficiency. Also, the Department of Energy estimates that you can save about 3% of your total gas bill over one year just by keeping your tires properly inflated. Check your tires at least once a month. You also save by prolonging the life of your tires and ultimately your engine. A franchised oil-change center usually can check your tires for you. Also check your wheel alignment regularly. Bad alignment can create very costly expenses if it is off and you don't get it fixed. Likewise, have your tires rotated once a year to prevent improper wear.

Park It, Buddy

Try to leave your car home as much as possible to reduce your overall maintenance costs. Walk or ride a bike whenever it's convenient—you'll save gas and get some exercise. If you must drive to work, try to carpool. Keeping the car in the garage more often also can help keep your car out of the shop.

Another gas saver is driving within the speed limit. The average household can save $45 per year just by obeying speed limit laws. For every mile per hour you go over the legal limit, you bring your fuel economy down by about 2%. Slow down and give yourself a break. Is it worth the wear and tear on your car, extra fuel, and possibly a speeding ticket to get somewhere a little earlier? I don't think so.

Mr. Fix-It

Where is the best place to have your car fixed? The dealer, a local mechanic, or a national chain? I don't recommend that you take it to a dealer. If you call around town to the different car dealers, you'll find that they are very expensive for even the most minor repairs. Dealers usually charge about 30% more than independent mechanics.

Many car owners are suckered into taking their car to the dealer, thinking the dealer provides better service or is the only one who can do the repairs properly. In reality, many independent mechanics can do just as good a job and charge much less. Car dealerships are slick marketers and get the majority of their customers from new car sales. A customer often can get used to bringing the car in for warranty checks and continue to bring the car in year after year.

I feel it's best to have your car repaired at a reputable local shop rather than a car dealership. Check your area to find the best independent mechanics. Auto part stores often can recommend experienced mechanics. Ask friends and relatives whether they have found a reliable local repair shop. Before leaving your car at the shop, ask for references and talk to regular customers. If people come back to the shop year after year, it's probably well run and provides good customer service. If you're lucky, you can find a shop that has great prices as well.

Getting the Maximum from a Gallon of Gas

Shell Oil once did a study where specially designed cars were able to get 400 miles per gallon. This feat was accomplished by minimizing resistance and drag, creating new engine designs, and using clever tricks to increase fuel economy. Of course, you cannot get this mileage in your ordinary car, but you can increase fuel efficiency in many other ways.

1. Keep your engine in good shape by having regular oil changes, once every 4,000 miles. Get a tune-up every year and a half to ensure that your engine is running at peak performance. Spark plugs and air filters are the number-one cause of lost engine efficiency, so replace them when needed. You can lose as much as two miles per gallon if the air filter or spark plugs are clogged or dirty. Think this is peanuts? You will save as much as $75 per year.

2. When you are looking to buy a new car, pay special attention to the EPA average miles per gallon. A car that gets just a few more miles to the gallon can save you several hundred dollars over the life of the car. Some of the most fuel-efficient cars on the road can get 58 miles to the gallon! The average for all cars is 28.1 miles per gallon. Hopefully you can find a car that gets results at least this good.

3. Don't use high-octane gas in your car unless your owner's manual specifies it. Studies have shown that mileage efficiency does not increase with the higher octane gasoline. Your car will run just fine with the cheaper stuff. Also, pump your own gas and pay cash when you can get discounts. You have no

reason to charge your gas with an oil charge card that features an outrageously high interest rate.

4. Never drive your car without first warming it up for about three minutes. A cold engine uses about 10% more gas. Also, if possible, avoid driving your car very short distances, such as to the neighbor's house or the mailbox down the street. Over a long period of time this puts undue wear and tear on your engine and your exhaust system.

5. Some people I know like to use their trunks as storage space. You pay to have extra weight back there. Take out all the tools and sports equipment and store them elsewhere. When you go on a trip, though, pack the trunk and other areas of the car as full as you can so you don't need to put a luggage carrier on top of the car. These devices can decrease fuel economy significantly.

Oily Mess

Ever had the problem of keeping your garage floor clean from oil and other car fluids? If you are tired of stains, try this special trick: Put paint thinner on top of the oil or fluid and then kitty litter on top of that. Give the litter a day or so to sop up the excess and then just sweep it up. You may need to use a few paper towels to finish off. Kitty litter works just as well as the expensive stuff you buy at the auto parts stores. Be very careful that no one smokes around the garage when you do this work; paint thinner is highly flammable.

Extend Your Antenna

Want to prolong the life of your car's power antenna? Twice a year, fully extend the antenna and clean it thoroughly with a strong grease-cutting cleaner or paint thinner. Then spray some *WD-40* or oil on it and move it up and down several times. Wipe off all the excess oil. Electric antennas often break on older cars simply because they are never cleaned and oiled.

ACTION LIST

1. If you are thinking about purchasing a new car, go to the local library and research the dealer's invoice cost through one of the consumer magazines.

    Date completed: _____

2. Sold on leasing your next car? Take all the lease documents to your banker so he or she can look them over and verify the numbers. Make sure you have a good working relationship with your banker so he or she doesn't just brush the lease off and try to get you to finance through them.

    Date completed: _____

3. When you sell your used car, get it in tip-top shape by detailing it inside and out and having it checked out mechanically. If there is anything wrong with it, have it fixed before you sell the car.

    Date completed: _____

4. If it has been more than 4,000 miles since your last oil change, have the oil changed immediately and begin to regularly change it.

    Date completed: _____

CHAPTER 7

Cut Insurance Costs but Not Coverage

Here's why insurance companies are mostly indestructible:
The cost of damages is most times less than the deductible.

—G. Sterling Leiby

What I hate about insurance is paying for something you hope you will never use. Unfortunately, we all need insurance in case those dreadful times do occur.

If you want to become a *$ensible $aver*, you need to learn the tricks to buying the right insurance, whether for your car, home, or health. You need to pay as little as possible but still get the coverage you need. How much coverage you need depends on your family status and financial situation. You should view insurance as a backup for those awful times, such as when the house has storm damage, 16-year-old Danny smashes up the family car, or your neighbor slips on your porch and breaks a leg.

If you shop smart, you can have all the coverage you need, often much more, and still keep your insurance costs low. In fact, it's not uncommon for people to take a hard look at their insurance coverage and trim costs to about half of what they presently pay. You can save and actually improve the quality of your insurance, too.

Life Insurance

Term for Endearment

Oh no, the insurance agent is coming! Yes, you need life insurance, but must you go through the ordeal of some pressured sales presentation? Hopefully, I can give you some pointers on life insurance that can prepare you for your next encounter with an agent.

First, I want to give you a short history of life insurance.

Ben Franklin was the first person to come up with the idea of mass-producing *death insurance*, as he called it. This name seems like the obvious title because you are buying insurance for when you die. If you die, the insurance company pays you.

But the guys who started to market the insurance realized quickly that no one would buy dismal *death insurance*. The insurers came up with the brilliant idea of calling it *life insurance*. That name sounded so much better to them. Of course, life insurance sold like hotcakes, and soon many insurance company coffers were overflowing with money.

The insurers' next idea was to get more money out of these people by lumping a low-interest investment with this life insurance. The insurance companies called it *whole life insurance* and sold it primarily to put more cash in the bank; the companies could invest the money at rates many times the rate of interest paid out on the policies.

The insurance companies in the business of protecting our families from financial ruin made an about-face into the investment business without us even knowing. The insurers were so successful at making money that when the great depression hit, and everything from the stock market to banks failed, insurance companies bailed out all the major institutions, providing loans at horrific rates of interest. Today, insurance companies are still quietly the most influential companies in the world, having billions more in assets than any other industry.

What's the moral of this story? For starters, *never*, and I mean *never*, buy insurance as an investment unless you want to contribute to an insurance company's portfolio. Any whole life or universal life policy that you buy is costing you much more in fees and lost interest than you should be paying. The world is full of far better-quality investments than an insurance policy. You should buy insurance for one reason: to protect your loved ones in case something disastrous happens to you. Insurance representatives aren't stupid. They know what it takes for you to sign on the dotted line, and they pray they can scare you enough to do it.

Don't fall for accidental death coverage or insurance for the kids. The chances that you'll die in an accident are very small, and your children do not need insurance, unless you would feel good about getting a check in the event one of them dies. The only life (or should I say *death* in honor of Ben) insurance you should buy is straight death coverage called term insurance. Get annually renewable term insurance and make sure it is guaranteed, which means that if your medical condition changes, the insurer still must renew your policy. If you are under age 50, I believe the best amount of insurance to own is about five to six times your gross annual salary. This would provide enough insurance for your family to maintain its lifestyle. If you're a two-income family, both partners should be insured. If one spouse stays at home to take care of children, it might be a good idea to have him or her insured for an amount to cover the costs of day care if he or she were to die. Finally, if you are over age 50, you need to evaluate whether you even need life insurance if you have substantial assets.

Life Insurance Switch

I generally advise not to cash in a cash-value life insurance policy and switch it with another if you have had the policy for more than seven years. If you have held the policy that long, chances are you have already paid tremendous fees. Most cash-value (whole life or universal life) policies have fees that disappear after this period of time, and the premiums begin to flatten out. Don't get the impression I mean you should run out and buy a cash-value policy. If you need more insurance, I advocate buying a term life policy for pure death protection.

Kiddie Insurance

Whatever you do, don't insure your child with his or her own life insurance policy. Insurance agents give you all sorts of reasons to insure children such as paying for their funeral, providing guaranteed insurance after they go to college, or using the policy to build a college fund. Hogwash. If you want to provide your child with money for college through life insurance, make sure that you and your spouse have plenty of coverage so if either of you die, your child can afford to finish college. Paying for insurance for a child is the same as throwing your money out the window.

Whole Life Insurance: Dump It or Keep It?

Most insurance companies pay their salespeople very well to sell life insurance. Some companies pay as much as the entire first year's premium in up-front commission to their sales force. How can they get away with this? Simple: The salespeople charge you. It's no wonder the insurance salesperson comes knocking on the door to see if you want to upgrade your policy. He or she knows it means another juicy payday.

You need to become *insurance-aware* to recognize when someone is just looking for a commission or is steering you in the right direction. Use the following information to arm yourself so you can decide if you need to keep your whole life policy:

1. If you are having difficulty coming up with the money every month to pay the premiums, you are probably paying too much. Whole life insurance can cost a fortune, especially if you are older. Term policies are generally much cheaper, which makes the payments easier. Again, never buy life insurance as an investment but only as death protection for your family.

2. If you have had your whole life policy for many years and the premiums have dropped considerably, consider keeping the policy. By now, you have paid many of the fees associated with the policy and can receive adequate benefits.

3. Make sure the return you are receiving on your savings portion of the policy is consistent with competitive bank CD rates.

4. Check several insurance companies in your area to compare rates. Many companies rely on the talents of their sales force to sell overpriced policies. If you know the competitive prices, you can approach your current insurance agent and have your premium reduced.

5. If you know you don't have enough coverage and find you cannot afford more with your current whole life policy, consider canceling your policy and shopping for a cheaper alternative. Or consider keeping the policy and getting term coverage as a supplement. At a minimum, have coverage that is at least five times the breadwinner's salary and about half of that for a non-working spouse.

6. Keep tabs on the financial well-being of your insurance company. Call the company once a year and ask for its annual report. Take a look at the balance sheet to determine whether

the company is profitable. If you smell something fishy, you can call your state's insurance commissioner and ask about the company's solvency.

Special note: If you decide to cancel any insurance policy for any reason, wait until your new policy is in force before you cancel the old one.

Buy Now

If you have been holding off buying term life insurance, then now is the time to buy. New laws are going into effect across the country that will make life insurance more expensive and will require insurers to set aside large cash reserves to make sure the money is available for claims. These reserves will directly impact the bottom-line profits of the insurance companies. Rates are probably as low now as they ever will be. Look for guaranteed annually renewable term policies or level term policies. Level term may be better because you can lock in a rate for 10 or 15 years, which protects you from major rate increases.

How to Calculate Your Life Insurance Needs

I have put together what I feel is a very comprehensive and precise formula to help you figure out exactly how much life insurance you should have. I urge you to take the time to fill out the following worksheet, especially if you aren't absolutely certain you have enough insurance. My experience is that most people are grossly underinsured. If your calculations prove that you need more insurance, purchase only guaranteed annually renewable term life insurance. Some 10- and 15-year term policies can be a good buy if you are guaranteed a rate lock for that period.

Instructions for the Life Insurance Formula

Capital Needs

Funeral expenses—you will need to estimate. A reasonable figure might be $5,000.

Final expenses—current bills that must be paid: charge accounts, etc.

Medical expenses—those not ordinarily covered by insurance.

Capital Needs

Funeral expenses   _____

Final expenses (current bills)   _____

Medical expenses not covered by insurance   _____

Estate taxes   _____

Attorney and court fees   _____

Emergency fund   _____

Pay off mortgage balance   _____

Education fund   _____

Other   _____

Total Capital Needs   _____ (A)

Capital Available

Liquid assets (checking and savings)   _____

Existing insurance proceeds* (company insurance
and personal policies if paid in lump sum)   _____

Death benefits of retirement programs
(if paid in lump sum)   _____

Other   _____

Total Capital Available   _____ (B)

*Proceeds can be taken in a lump sum or in installment
payments.

Annual Income Needs of Survivors

Spouse, children   _____

Other (parents)   _____

Total Annual Income Needs of Survivors   _____ (C)

Annual Income Available to Survivors

Social Security survivors' benefits   _____

Survivors' benefits from retirement programs
(if paid in installments)   _____

continued

Spouse's wage   _____

Income from investments   _____

Other (teenage children, veterans)   _____

Total Annual Income Available   _____ (D)

Calculations to Determine Total Amount of Life Insurance Needed

1. Total Capital Needs   _____ (A)

   Less Total Capital Available   _____ (B)

   = Net Capital Needs   _____ (E)

2. Total Annual Income Needs   _____ (C)

   Less Total Annual Income Available   _____ (D)

   = Net Annual Income Needs   _____ (F)

3. Additional Capital Needed   _____ (G)

   Divide (F) by the return assumed on the invested capital. For example, at an annual return rate of 10%, you would need $90,000 to generate an annual income of $9,000. At an 8% annual return, you would need $112,500 to generate the same annual income of $9,000 ($9,000 divided by .08 = $112,500).

4. Total Additional Life Insurance Needed
   (Add (E) and (G))   _____ (G)

Estate taxes—costs will vary from state to state. It's best to consult with an estate-planning attorney or financial planner for assistance.

Attorney and court fees—seek assistance as noted above.

Emergency fund—estimate a minimum of three months fixed living expenses.

Pay-off mortgage balance—If this is desirable, list current balance.

Education fund—estimate the amount necessary to complete four years of college for each child.

Other—would include a major expense or debt not mentioned above (for example, pay off auto loan).

Capital Available

Liquid assets—total of funds in savings and checking accounts.

Existing insurance proceeds—list total of all insurance proceeds from either group (employer-paid plans) or individual policies.

Death benefits—includes IRAs and company retirement plans that make a lump-sum distribution in the event of death.

Other—would include help from relatives or investments that could be liquidated, such as stocks and bonds.

Annual Income Needs

Spouse, children—estimate the amount necessary to maintain a comfortable standard of living.

Other—estimate the amount necessary to support a parent or relative.

Annual Income Available

Social Security survivors' benefits—your local Social Security office can provide you with this information.

Survivors' benefit from retirement programs—if benefits are paid in installments rather than a lump sum, list the annual amount.

Spouse's wage—if surviving spouse is employed, list annual income.

Income from investments—interest, dividends, etc.

Other—any other source of income such as veteran's benefits or money earned by teenage children.

Calculations

1. Total Capital Needs—take Total Capital Needs (A) and subtract Total Capital Available (B), which will equal Net Capital Needs (E).

2. Total Annual Income Needs—Take Total Annual Income Needs (C) and subtract Annual Income Available (D), which will equal Annual Income Needs (F).

3. Additional Capital Needed—Divide the Net Annual Income Needs (F) by the interest rate you assume you could receive on your investments. The lower the assumed interest rate, the greater the amount of investment funds needed.

4. Total Additional Life Insurance Needs—By adding Net Capital Needs (E) and Additional Capital Needed (G), you will arrive at a figure representing the amount of insurance (if any) needed to make up the shortage or deficiency in capital to maintain an adequate standard of living and provide for those things requiring a significant cash outlay.

Auto Insurance

Collision Decision

Drop your collision and comprehensive auto insurance coverage if your car is more than five years old or is worth less than $1,500. Collision is often the most expensive portion, and eliminating it saves you 50% or more on the yearly premium. The charges you would incur to repair an accident's damage probably would not justify the extra amount you pay in premiums. Make sure you don't drop your liability coverage though, because it protects you if you cause an accident and hurt someone. If you have a bad accident, your insurer can pay you what he or she thinks the car is worth, which is often much less than you think it is worth. After subtracting the deductible, you could be left with a pittance.

Fill the Gap

If you lease a car, look into the possibility of gap insurance. This coverage protects you if the car is significantly damaged or totaled in an accident. The insurance covers the difference between what the insurance company gives you for the accident and what is actually owed on the car, which is often significantly more. Many leasing companies offer gap insurance, but you need to ask about it. Banks and credit unions rarely provide this insurance unless you specifically request it.

A Quick $80

Want to save at least $80 today by making one phone call? Pick up the phone and call your insurance company. Ask the insurer to raise the deductible on your car insurance to $500 or $1,000. Keeping your deductible under $500 is costing you a lot extra in insurance payments and is making the insurance company rich.

The extra savings will make up for any losses you incur if you're in an accident. If you're afraid you won't have the extra money around if you get in an accident, use a credit card to bail you out of the emergency. Do not give the insurance company more money than you need to.

Eliminate overlapping coverage. For instance, don't pay extra for medical coverage if you have health insurance that covers your medical expenses in the event of an accident. Scrutinize your policies and eliminate the medical coverage if your auto policy covers it. You can save approximately 30% by dropping this needless expense.

Car Insurance Trap

Insurers in most states are not required to disclose their underwriting guidelines. As a result, most applicants don't know why they're rejected, and policyholders also don't know what's required to maintain their insurance. Many people unwittingly lose their coverage. If you feel you have been treated unfairly, contact your state's insurance commissioner. If your coverage was suspended, ask the commissioner to have your policy reinstated until the dispute is settled.

A couple of tips worth repeating:

- Take the highest deductible you feel comfortable with.
- Don't file small claims—this keeps the adjusters off your back. View car insurance as protection against major damage or loss.

Auto Insurance Suspension

Consider suspending your auto insurance coverage for any length of time you are not driving. If you are going on vacation for a couple of weeks, you can save money because you will not be driving during that period. Call your insurance agent to see if the company provides this option. Many companies do because senior citizens go on vacations often and have requested it.

Home Protection

Homeowner's insurance can leave you high and dry if you aren't well covered. Many unsuspecting consumers think they are completely covered for any losses if their insurance covers the whole house and all belongings. The reality is that most complete losses are not covered because homeowners opted for cheaper coverage. The best thing to do is assume your policy doesn't cover much. Determine the value of your home and possessions, then get coverage that insures 50% more than this value. Make sure you know the provisions of the policy, especially what's not covered. Buy supplemental coverage such as a personal items floater if you have valuables. Don't forget special coverage if you have your business in your home.

Rental Troubles

If you are a renter, be sure to have a renter's insurance policy that covers your belongings. These policies are usually inexpensive and protect quite a bit. With rising crime, apartments and town houses are easy targets. The insurance probably will pay off in the long run. If you have expensive possessions such as computers, jewelry, or fancy electronics, make sure the insurance company knows about these and has included a valuables rider in the policy.

Vacation Savings

You can cut insurance costs for a vacation home by purchasing a property that is readily accessible to fire and emergency services. If you buy a home that is in a remote spot, chances are your rates are dramatically higher. If you have valuables in your vacation home, make sure you keep them to a minimum. To lower your rates, do the following:

- Install fire and theft alarms hooked into a central monitoring location.
- Install a temperature alarm that sounds when temperatures get to the point where the pipes might burst.
- Install deadbolt locks, smoke detectors, and a fire extinguisher.
- Hire a caretaker or management company to watch your home when you are away.

Disability Protection

Disability insurance is often overlooked by many consumers because most insurance agents don't push it—they are too busy trying to sell you life insurance. Long-term disability coverage provides monthly benefits if you are injured or contract an illness that keeps you from earning an income. Your chances of being disabled are much greater than dying, especially if you are young or middle-aged. At about age 40, you are four times more likely to be injured than to die. Disability insurance can be invaluable because if you're unable to work, your family would no longer have your income.

Unfortunately, disability coverage is extremely expensive. Insurance can cost as much as $1,900 per year for a middle-aged man to get about $2,000 in monthly benefits. Also, Social Security's qualifications are very strict, and most company policies are very inadequate.

Some employer group policies don't cover you until you have worked for the company for several years; these policies also may have limits of up to $500 per month income replacement. Employer policies are primarily meant to supplement your own disability coverage.

If you're buying disability coverage, it's important to carefully evaluate what coverage you need. I would say that your coverage should equal about 60% to 70% of your gross pay. Your benefits should start 90 days after your disability occurs. This uncovered time (called the elimination period) is why you should have emergency savings to cover your expenses for the first three months. The coverage should continue until age 65 when you can get Social Security. Buy your disability insurance with after-tax dollars, making your income benefits tax-free.

It is very important to find a policy that defines disability specifically. Look for a policy that offers benefits if you are incapacitated and cannot work in your current occupation. Many policies try to deny your benefits if you can work in another occupation but don't want to. Also, insist on a guaranteed renewable policy, which means that the insurer cannot cancel your policy or increase your premiums. Also, make sure the company you select has an excellent reputation. Check with the insurance commissioner in your state about the company's past claims' performances.

If you are hesitant about the cost involved with your policy, the best way to lower your premiums is to extend the elimination period another three months. Your cost can come down by as much as 25%.

As with most insurance products, like cars, you have options. I recommend you look into a residual benefits provision that would pay a partial amount of your benefits if you could perform only a percentage of job functions but can still work. Read your policy carefully because some programs give you partial payments but only for a limited time, not to age 65.

Another good option is a cost of living adjustment. With this rider, the amount of your benefits increases yearly as the cost of living increases. This increase is usually determined by the insurance company.

Make sure you are truthful when you fill out your application. You need to reveal any conditions that may affect your ability to get the coverage. Believe me, insurance companies are sticklers for things such as smoking, drinking, and any medical problems. Insurers may not bother you while you're paying the premiums, but if anything happens and they need to start paying you, they will do thorough investigations. If the insurer finds any inconsistencies, say good-bye to the payout. Don't try to get policies from two different companies. The insurers have a way of finding out, and they generally won't pay if you are receiving duplicate payouts.

Answers to Tough Insurance Questions

Of all the questions I am asked as *The $ensible $aver*, insurance is the hottest topic. This interest makes sense because insurance is confusing, and you can get in trouble if you don't know what you are buying. Become educated and ask many questions of your insurance agent. Some commonly asked questions are answered here:

If I rent, am I covered by the apartment complex's policy?

Unfortunately for you, landlords are required only to have insurance on the property and general liability coverage in case someone is injured on the grounds. You are best off purchasing your own renter's coverage for personal possessions and liability if someone has an accident inside your apartment. Rates vary from company to company, so check around.

Should I insure my house for the market price or replacement cost?

In most areas of the country, the best approach is to insure the house for its replacement value rather than market value. Replacement policies are generally less expensive. Part of the market cost in your home is the land, so if your house burns to the ground or a tornado blows it away, the land is still around. You can dig a new foundation, so you have no reason to pay the extra premium to insure the land. A guaranteed replacement policy is your best bet.

Do I have to pay an extra premium if my son or daughter drives my car?

Absolutely. If your children are in an accident and you have not notified the insurance company, you can be denied payment on the accident and lose your coverage. For full protection, call your insurance company and tell them if anyone under age 21 is driving the car.

What should I do if I can't find a life insurance policy of a relative who has died and left me beneficiary?

Don't fret. If you know the name of the company that issued the policy, simply contact the insurer and explain the situation. You will usually have no problem if you prove your identity and relationship to your relative.

If you have no clue about the name of the company, contact the American Council of Life Insurance, 1001 Pennsylvania Ave. NW, Washington, DC 20004. Ask for a policy search form and include a self-addressed, stamped envelope with your request. This organization will contact the 100 largest life insurance companies in the country. Most likely, the insurance policy will be with one of these companies. After you find the company, you can write to collect on the policy.

Can I buy flood insurance for my house?

If you are in an area sanctioned by the Flood Disaster Protection Act, you can buy flood insurance. About 20,000 communities in the United States qualify under this Act. Contact the Federal Insurance Commission at 500 C St. SW, Washington, DC 20472 to find out if your area qualifies. Most houses can be insured for replacement cost plus any household property.

I hear all this talk about Medicare cuts lately. How expensive is "Medi-gap" insurance? Should I protect myself with it?

"Medi-gap" coverage pays for the part of your hospital stay that regular Medicare coverage does not. If you are currently eligible for Medicare payments, you should have Medi-gap coverage. This insurance generally costs about $800 to $1,000 per year. Be diligent in your search for good Medi-gap coverage because many policies have loopholes that exclude portions of payments. Go to an independent insurance agent who has access to several different companies. (For more detailed information on Health Insurance, see Chapter 12.)

Do I lose my health insurance benefits the day I leave my job?

If you quit your job or are terminated, your coverage continues for 18 months under the umbrella of COBRA (Consolidated Omnibus Reconciliation Act). This law enables you to remain in the employer's health insurance group as long as you make the premium payments calculated for that group. After 18 months, you can continue payments, but usually at a higher price.

Is long-term health-care insurance expensive?

Long-term health-care coverage pays for nursing care in an institution or your home. Premiums are based on your age, the daily amount the policy pays, and the waiting period before you receive care in your home or enter an institution. Most policies take effect about 30 days after you start receiving care and pay about $75 per day. Policy premiums range from $500 per year to well over $3,000 depending on your age. Yes, these policies are expensive, but they're well worth it in the long run.

ACTION LIST

1. If you do not currently have life insurance, fill out the life insurance worksheet in this chapter and purchase term insurance for the calculated amount.

   Date completed: _____

2. If you currently have any form of whole life insurance, pull the policy out and review the fine print. Use the guidelines discussed in this chapter to determine whether you are paying too much.

   Date completed: _____

3. Call your car insurance agent today and raise your deductible to $500. You will save on premiums and still be fully protected.

   Date completed: _____

4. Check into the possibility of purchasing disability insurance coverage, especially if you are in a job where the likelihood of getting injured is great.

   Date completed: _____

5. If you rent, purchase a special renter's policy from your insurance agent to cover you in case you are burglarized or anyone has an accident on the premises.

   Date completed: _____

CHAPTER 8

$ensible Education Moves

> In my opinion, education is an investment in the future and never an unwanted expense.
>
> —Mark W. Miller

The great dream of sending kids to the best colleges has become an impossibility for many American families. The average cost of sending a child to college for four years is about $70,000, and twice as much at some Ivy League schools such as Harvard and Yale. Unfortunately, these costs will continue to rise and are likely to double every decade.

While college can cost a bundle, you don't have to pay all the high costs associated with higher education. As long as you know how to take advantage of cost-cutting opportunities that abound on the college campuses, you can reduce your costs significantly.

One of the greatest ways to finance college is through student loans. The government loans and gives away billions of dollars every year to help students pay for college. The best way to get some of this money is to make yourself seem as needy as possible. Obviously, you don't want to quit your job to qualify for these funds. But you may want to position assets so that you have less available cash. For instance, you may want to pay down your mortgage, or contribute more to retirement plans. This is not dishonest;

it is simply smart money management. If you need help paying for college expenses, you've got to be creative.

Can I Afford to Send My Kids to College?

Parents may say that sending their kids to college is their number one priority and is even more important than saving for retirement. The reality is that about 90% of parents do not have a savings program for their children's college education. It's no wonder many children only get a high school education. Their parents just didn't save.

Sometimes, the problem is that the parents never made enough money to save, but more often, parents simply don't know how costly college is and how to save for a long-term goal such as education.

If your child or grandchild is depending on your help to pay for his or her college education, you shouldn't focus on saving every last penny to pay for all of the education. You should, however, be in the position to pay for a large percentage of the costs if you want your child to have a top-notch education. Plan to pay for room, board, and books and let the child pick up the tab for extracurricular activities.

How much do you need to save? The average cost for four years at a public college will be about $125,000 in about 15 years. The cost for a private school will be about $250,000. This is enough to make your knees knock. The reality is that you will probably be able to come up with only about 50% to 60% of the money your child will need to cover the cost of college. Most likely, you will also have to take out several loans to cover all the college expenses. The important thing is to start saving now if you want to contribute even partially to their education. Believe me, the partial contribution that you make will be extremely important as education costs continue to rise.

A general guideline to help you save is to sock away $2 per day for a newborn child. For every five years closer your child gets to college, triple this amount. For instance, if your child is five, you should be saving $6 per day. If he or she is ten, you should save $12 per day, etc. How much and how often you save is purely up to you. A recent study by the Association for Financial Planning concluded that most families pay about 27% of college expenses.

This figure would be much higher if more Americans would p[ ]
ahead by setting up a savings program.

One consideration is whether the child will go to a public or priv[ ]
institution. Plan to pay about double the cost if Junior choose[ ]
private school. A good compromise is for your child to go to an in[ ]
pensive local college or community college for a year or two a[ ]
then transfer to an expensive private college to earn a diplom[ ]
After all, a resume will list the school someone graduates fro[ ]
right?

If you haven't started to save for your children's college educati[ ]
by the time they have hit high school, be prepared for a strugg[ ]
To pay for a good portion of a public school, you'll need to sa[ ]
about $600 per month. You better start early.

What I'm talking about is making choices. If you choose to not sa[ ]
your options on what type of college your kids attend and ul[ ]
mately the quality of their education are greatly diminished. I[ ]
best to have all your options open so that the child can do what [ ]
or she really wants to.

There's one other reason why it's absolutely imperative to make [ ]
significant contribution to your children's education: to set a[ ]
example that they will not forget. If you are not serious about suc[ ]
an important savings matter, it's likely that your child will not b[ ]
serious about college. Talk about how you are saving for colleg[ ]
and encourage your kids to save also. Emphasize how important [ ]
is to work toward a family goal—their education.

Hundreds of thousands of young men and women cannot mak[ ]
their student loan payments and have bad credit. While some stu[ ]
dent loan defaults are legitimate hardships, in thousands o[ ]
instances, however, students just plain didn't pay up on thei[ ]
loans because they don't care about making good on their loa[ ]
obligations. It is the parent's responsibility to instill these value[ ]
and part of our task as parent-teachers is to take on responsibil[ ]
ity ourselves and help our children with the most vital of all thing[ ]
. . . education.

Prepaid College

Yes, believe it or not, there are many colleges that now offer prepaid
college tuition plans. Most of these plans allow you to lock in cur[ ]
rent tuition costs if you pay in advance of your child attending the[ ]

an

lent must meet minimum admittance requirements
:hool.

te
 a
x-
id
.a.
n,

th these plans is once you sign on the dotted line,
ommitted to going to that school. What happens
its to go to a different school other than your alma
e your money. Maybe this particular college doesn't
s that your child is looking for and wants. You also
em of knowing whether prepayment of tuition will
t protection in the long run. It could be a poor way
money.

>n
e.
ve

tion can seem attractive by freeing you of the
ng process down the road. However, there are too
s with a prepaid plan, including the fact that the col-
se may no longer exist in 15 years, or it may have
tantially.

e,
i-
's
e

olleges that pioneered these plans are no longer offer-
e reason is that they had difficulties investing the
ough to preserve the capital for when it was needed.
ans, you are basically giving your money to the insti-
est. Remember, these academics are in the business
 not investing, so they might not do as good of a job
ir money as you could yourself.

a
n
h
e
,
t

ldren choose their own college or you'll risk a major
ur relationship with them. You could also lose all your
if they choose another institution and the college you
iose won't refund your money or even your investment

e
-
f
r
t

et is to begin a college savings fund for each of your chil-
it money into that plan on a regular basis. A lump sum
would work well. I recommend that you invest in a
tual fund for a long-term goal such as education. When
ear or two from using the money, preserve the capital in
ile investment.

nother type of prepayment that makes a lot of sense.
ges allow students to prepay all four years of college the
hey enroll. This locks in current costs for tuition, room
, and other expenses. Many colleges make loans available
these plans. With this arrangement, you don't have the
ssures of choosing a school for your kids years before
ady. If you take advantage of this plan, ask about your
 refund if the student changes schools or drops out
e four years.

If you decide to use one of these types of plans, before you make your final decision, look at the upfront costs compared to what you could make by investing that money elsewhere.

College Freebies

Enrolling in an accredited course at a local university or community college is a great way to get the use of student privileges. A student ID card can get you into the gym free, which is much cheaper than joining the local health club. Use the school library, obtain free entrance into some school events, receive cheap rates on university movies, productions, sporting events, and possibly obtain free health services. Don't forget all the things you can use a student ID for around town: movies, plays, concerts. Enroll in a class you truly will enjoy and consider your student ID a fringe benefit.

School Clothes

When it's time to send the kids back to school with new clothes, donate their old ones to charity. It means a tax deduction for you. If you give away items valued at $1,500, then you can take a tax deduction of over $500. This isn't chump change. Don't trash old clothes when someone else's kids can get some wear out of them and you can make some money to boot.

How to Choose the Best Educational Online Service

Computers are here to stay, whether you like them or not. Computers are revolutionizing the way the world does business. If you refuse to learn about them or think they're over-rated, you'll probably be left in the dust.

One of the fastest growing segments of the computer revolution are online services. Installing a modem in your computer allows you to access huge data banks offering services to help you at home and the office. They contain information on personal finance, travel, games, hobbies, sports, leisure, e-mail, and online chat (you can talk to fellow computer users *live* via your keyboard). I've listed some of the more popular services and a brief evaluation of each:

- America Online (1-800-827-6364): The costs are $9.95 per month for five hours of access and $2.95 for each additional hour. America Online is the fastest growing service today. The costs are reasonable and America Online offers many diverse services.

  You'll find the travel, sports, and leisure services extremely helpful. The "bulletin boards" are fun. These live, online conversations between subscribers on the system are interesting, entertaining, and informative.

  I found the investing and finance sections to be very basic, providing very few in-depth financial tools. At times, it can be difficult to get a connection to the Internet, but this problem is short-term.

- CompuServe (1-800-848-8199): The costs are $9.95 a month for unlimited basic service access plus three hours of access to the Internet. CompuServe offers more services than any of its competitors. It's easy to use, but beware of add-on pricing for some types of information.

  The investing and finance sections are great. The basic services are better than the competition's. Travel, database, and sports and leisure are also very good.

  CompuServe offers the most comprehensive service of the lot. I recommend this service for a more seasoned computer user.

- Prodigy (1-800-776-3449): The costs are $9.95 per month for five hours and $2.95 for each additional hour. The graphics are a little lacking. It's not as user-friendly as the other services. Advertising is everywhere, which I find frustrating. On a more positive note, they do provide some top-notch services.

Microsoft has introduced a new online service called The Microsoft Network (MSN), but up to this point it is still very small compared to the others. Give Mr. Gates a few years and he is sure to give the rest a run for their money.

One thing I haven't discussed is how to connect to the Internet. You can access the World Wide Web (a fancy term for the easiest way to browse the Internet) through any of the online services. However, you can save some cash by bypassing these online services if you have a bit of computer savvy. I recommend calling an Internet service provider and hooking up directly to the Net. Most major cities have providers. Check the Yellow Pages. An Internet service provider will give you the software you need for direct access, and you will have no online service to mess with. Make sure the service has a local access number so you won't be paying long-distance rates to be connected.

A word of caution about the Internet: It is still difficult to navigate through the Net, even with today's software. If you don't possess some computer knowledge or don't like to spend a lot of time on computers, the Net may not be for you. However, it won't be long, perhaps by the year 2000, that several hundred million people will be on the Internet. I believe by then it will be so easy to navigate and information will be so accessible that the Internet service providers might just put the national online services out of business.

ACTION LIST

1. Evaluate your family's need for college funds. If you have more than one child, you could be in for a major shock come college time if you have not been saving. Start a savings plan today if you haven't already.

    Date completed: _____

2. To save on many different services around your area and get some education in the process, enroll in a college course. You will be eligible to receive student discounts on many services at the school and can take advantage of student discounts throughout your town.

    Date completed: _____

3. If you want to become more educated about computers and take advantage of the vast research capability of databases around the world, consider subscribing to one of many online services.

    Date completed: _____

CHAPTER 9

Saving Around the Home and Office

> Beware of little expenses . . . a small leak will sink a mighty ship.
>
> —Ben Franklin

Yes, the home is where the heart is, and the office is where you often lose that heart. The last thing you should be worrying about is how you are going to keep the house in good order and also keep your job.

In this chapter, I want to give you some tips and strategies that will hopefully help take some of the money pressure off you so that you can focus on living a much more relaxing life. So when you are trying to keep up with the Joneses and the person in the cubicle next to you at work, you might just have a slight advantage because you're armed with a few tricks.

Digital Savings

Invest in a programmable thermostat for your home. Department of Energy studies have proven that a homeowner can save as much as 25% on home heating and cooling just by having the thermostat a few degrees higher or lower for a portion of every day. You can purchase a good programmable thermostat on sale at a discount home supply store for as little as $35.

Mother Nature's Heating and Cooling

Use nature's own heating and cooling system to your advantage. In most parts of the country, nights are cool about nine months out of the year. If you want to cool the house, open the windows at night and let the cool, fresh air circulate through your house. An attic fan will dramatically increase air flow. In the morning and afternoon, close the curtains and shades on the sunny side of your home. Keep the windows on the "dark side" of the house open for air circulation. If it's cold outside and you want to keep the house warm, keep your windows shut. Keep your curtains, blinds and shades shut until the sun comes out, and then open them to let the sun warm the house. When the sun sets, shut them again to keep the house warm. If you pay more attention to nature's ways, you can save substantially.

Drafty Blues

Test your home for airtight problems at least once a year. Check around windows, doors, and any cracks that you might discover. Caulk both the interior and exterior surfaces that you know are causing problems. After you caulk these areas, you may find that other leaks develop primarily due to reshifting of the drafts, so check again. Weather-stripping can be a good way to seal up the air leaks around doors. Caulking and weather-stripping don't take much time or money and can save you as much as 10% on your heating and cooling bill.

Turn Off the Lights

Turn off decorative outside gas or electric lamps when you can unless they are used for safety purposes. A couple of gas lights that burn year round can use up enough gas to heat an entire house for a winter! Depending on the part of the country you live in, it can cost as much as $4 per month to keep that flame aglow. If you have to have outdoor lighting, buy an inexpensive timer or photocell that will turn the lights on and off automatically.

Water Drips

A few water saving tips: Fix leaks fast. A running toilet can use as much as 2000 gallons of water a year. I know since I once mistakenly let a broken toilet run on for about a week. My water bill doubled. Avoid watering the lawn during the day when the sun just dries it up. Dusk is the best time to water. Tell your family not to let the water run while shaving, brushing teeth, washing dishes, or cleaning clothes by hand.

Toilets and Shower Heads That Save Bucks

Did you know toilet flushing represents the greatest demand on the country's water supply? It accounts for about 38% of all the water consumed! For decades, the normal toilet used 5 gallons per flush. In the late 1970s, manufacturers introduced the so-called water-conserving toilet that used 3.5 gallons per flush. Not a big difference. The newest toilets use only 1.5 gallons of water per flush. Most new toilets are inexpensively priced and have the same type of performance records.

Water and sewer rates vary widely from city to city, but it is probably safe to say you could easily save $50 a year per toilet by using low-flow toilets in your home. That may not seem like much; however, you must remember you are conserving water that could be vital to your community. If you replace old toilets with new ones, they should pay for themselves within three to four years. If your toilets are more than 20 years old, you might think about replacing them anyway because they are probably becoming less efficient.

Showers consume more than one-fifth of all the water used indoors and more hot water than any other fixture or appliance. Installing a low-flow shower head is a simple and inexpensive way to cut down on water consumption.

For approximately $10 per shower installed in your home, the average family can save about 10,000 gallons of water per year, plus the energy it takes to heat part of that water, which can run about $30 to $60 per year. Of course, savings will depend on how often your family uses the shower, what kind of shower heads you currently own, and how much you pay for heating your water.

It used to be that shower heads usually delivered about 5 to 8 gallons of water per minute. Manufacturers have recently done a good job of cutting back the flow rates and not lowering the quality of the shower spray. Shower heads designed for low water flow usually have a smaller spray area and might also mix air with the flow to provide more pressure. Most new shower heads deliver about 3 gallons of water per minute. Quite an improvement.

Installing a new shower head is simple. This usually means removing the old shower head with large pliers or an adjustable wrench. If it is stuck, steady the pipe with a pipe wrench while you turn the head. Then simply screw the new head into place.

A Flip of the Switch

Most people think it's sensible to turn the lights off in a room when you leave. Sounds right, doesn't it? The truth is turning a regular incandescent light off and on shortens the life of the bulb. If you are leaving the room only for a few minutes and are an obsessive light switch flipper, think twice about flipping that switch. You'll be better off leaving the light on and coming back in a few minutes. If you have fluorescent bulbs, it's a different ball game. Fluorescent bulbs are the most efficient of all lighting sources—so efficient that you can probably leave the room for several hours and the lights still will not have consumed much electricity. Also, fluorescent bulbs are stronger and are not as prone to burning out from excessive switch flipping.

Light It Right

Think those long-life light bulbs are a lifesaver? Think again. Avoid long-life bulbs except for hard-to-reach places. They cost more and are less energy efficient than normal light bulbs. Buy generic bulbs at the grocery store or discount home supply store. You'll be much better off.

Burn, Baby, Burn

If you build a fire and burn wood often in the winter, consider a new twist. During the summer months, roll your used newspapers into tight logs and tie them with cord. For best results, wet the paper before you begin rolling. Let the logs sit for a few months, and when winter rolls around, you have recycled logs. You'll appreciate the news all over again as you sit by your politically correct fire. Al Gore will love ya!

Exhausted Dryer

Keep your dryer exhaust vent clean and clear of debris to help your dryer run as efficiently as possible. If your vent is clogged, it can reduce the ability of your dryer to dry clothes properly. It's similar to having a clogged lint screen. Check the vent at least once every six months to make sure it's not full of lint.

Heater Checkup

Annual heating and cooling checkups save money in the long run. Although an inspection costs about $40, you'll lose even more money if your system is malfunctioning or you have improper air-flow in your home. Call a respected heating and cooling company to inspect your systems at least once a year. You will be more comfortable in your home and your equipment will last many more years.

Appliance Reliance

We've become a society dependent on the modern conveniences, so it's best to keep your timesaving appliances in good shape. Once a year, check the seals around refrigerator and freezer doors. Cracked or broken seals mean your refrigerator has to work a lot harder. Keep the dust bag in your vacuum clean. If it is full, the vacuum loses its suction and is less efficient. Don't forget to change the furnace filter every 3–6 months. These can get clogged fast. Keep the drains in your dishwasher clear; clogged drains can cause your machine to malfunction or overflow. All these easy maintenance procedures can save you a lot of money over the years.

Cold Air Flow

Have you had the freon in your air conditioner checked lately? If the hot summer months are approaching, it may be a good time to have the freon checked by a qualified professional. If it is low, your air conditioner could work twice as hard to cool your home. We all know how much electricity they can use. This is one of the tasks that I don't recommend you do yourself because of the dangers associated with freon. Call in an expert if it's been several years since you've had your air conditioner checked.

Energy-Efficient Appliances

You can really save a bundle with many of the new energy-efficient appliances on the market. The following is information from the Council for an Energy-Efficient Economy. It gives average annual savings figures if you use regular appliances as opposed to energy-efficient models.

Annual Operating Cost:		
	Average Appliance	*Energy-Efficient Appliance*
Central air conditioner:	$300	$150
Window air conditioner:	60	40
Electric clothes dryer:	70	55
Gas clothes dryer:	30	25
Clothes washer:	90	45
Dishwasher:	70	45
Frost-free freezer:	135	75
Manual-defrost freezer:	75	40
Household light fixtures:	75	25-50
Frost-free refrigerator:	120	70
Manual-defrost refrigerator:	45	30
Electric stove:	60	50
Gas stove:	45	35
Television:	25	10
Electric water heater:	300	150
Gas water heater:	160	130

Hot Frig

If at all possible, try to locate your refrigerator away from the dishwasher or stove. Both the dishwasher and the stove radiate heat that can cause your refrigerator to run harder. If the refrigerator must be next to one of these appliances, put some kind of insulation between them.

Condenser Tune-up

Cleaning the condenser coils on your older refrigerator can save you a lot of money in the long run. The coils are hard to get at behind the refrigerator, but if you clean them once a year you will save on service calls, and your refrigerator will run more efficiently and longer. Simply roll your refrigerator out from the wall and vacuum the coils. By cleaning the coils, air flows more easily and overheating problems can be avoided.

Leaky Freezer

Is your refrigerator or freezer door's gasket tight? To check, simply put a 150 watt outdoor flood light inside your refrigerator and turn it on. With the kitchen light off, close the door and look for light coming out. A poor gasket seal can often be fixed simply by adjusting the leveling legs on the bottom of the refrigerator. If this doesn't work, then you will need to replace the gasket seals. Having the seals tight can save on your energy bills.

A Garage Sale Bonanza

'Tis always the season to be rummaging—through the closets, that is. Spring and fall may be the best times for a garage sale since the cool air tends to make it easier for money to flow from buyers' pocketbooks. Why not do it, since you've been putting it off for years?

A garage sale is a great way to get rid of some of the clutter in your life and add to your bank account. When tromping through the attic and other storage areas in your house, look for some of these "hot" items: old books, desks, tables and chairs, toys, big band records, pictures (people like frames), garden tools, and sporting goods. These items sell like lemonade at a summer Little League game.

Forget selling clothes; it's a real pain trying to sort and price them all. Save these for Goodwill or the Salvation Army and take a tax deduction at the end of the year.

Unless you live in Beverly Hills, there is no use in trying to get big bucks for your used items. Sell all your items at what you might think is about 70% off retail. A simple pricing system is to price everything in round numbers like $.50, $1, $2, etc. It makes figuring much easier. None of this $.99 stuff. Again, you're not a retail store. Get a bunch of different colored stickers and use them to denote the different prices and post a color-coded sign on the wall so that people can see the prices. Most garage sale junkies think this is a clever system. For more expensive or unique items, just mark the price right on them.

To make a garage sale successful, you have to advertise. Put an ad in the most popular paper around your area and also some more localized shopper papers. The best days to have your sale are Thursday through Sunday, with the weekend obviously being the highest volume days. Your ad should be eye-catching with a lead line such as "The mother of all sales" (a little exaggerating never hurts). In the ad, mention your top two or three items. You'll also need to post neon-colored signs all around the neighborhood. Also, you can make a family project of passing out 100 or so flyers around the block. You will be surprised at how many neighbors will show up.

When the day arrives for the big sale, have a couple of bargain tables with very low prices on them and a sign saying something like "everything's a quarter." This works great for small items you want to go fast.

Anything left over from your sale can go to Goodwill or the Salvation Army. Another tax deduction.

A Chef at Hand

After barbecuing on a charcoal grill, close or cover all vents in the grill, both on the top and bottom of the grill. This will cause the remaining charcoal to burn out. For the next grilling, shake the grill a bit to loosen the ash from the charcoal, add a few more briquettes of charcoal, then light as usual. A bag of charcoal lasts about three times longer than if you let the charcoal burn itself up each time. This is a great idea for avid barbecuers. Barbecuing can be fun, and it's great when the cooking is done and there are no pots and pans to clean. Try using tin foil with the edges folded up for grilling your vegetables alongside your hot dogs and hamburgers. This eliminates more clean up and gives a great taste to veggies.

Leather Weather

Any leather items you have in the house should be cleaned at least once a year to help them weather use and abuse. This would include shoes, jackets, purses, and even automobile seats. You can use saddle soap to clean them and finish off with a waterproofing spray. When you can, wear a scarf or some type of protection around the collar areas of a leather garment. The oils from your skin and hair can damage the leather surface. If you have difficulty cleaning the leather yourself, take it to a dry cleaner that specializes in leather. Proper care will make your leather products last much longer.

Shoe Tips

Invest in shoe trees to help your shoes last as long as possible. Shoe trees will also help to keep the shape of your shoes better. Cedar shoe trees are the best because they absorb odors and wetness. Make sure the shoe trees aren't too tight because they can cause the leather to stretch and crack. Also, preserve shoes by applying what is called Meltonian. It sells for about two bucks a bottle and will keep shoes soft and clean. Finally, you don't have to replace an entire heel on a shoe when just a small portion is worn. Ask for a "tap." A shoemaker can do this service in a couple of minutes for a few dollars, and the shoes will look and wear just fine.

Nature's Green Thing

With the debate about keeping the environment healthy raging at all-time highs, here are some tips to being environmentally conscious and saving money as well:

The key to accomplishing both is to reuse as many items in your household as possible. Instead of throwing things out, find new and creative ways to use them. When you have stretched the life of a product as long as you can, dispose of it in an environmentally sound way.

First, when it is possible, try to pick products that have long life spans. Disposable products such as razors, cameras, cups, plates, lighters, and diapers all end up in the same place—your local landfill. As an example, in the United States alone 500 million lighters are tossed out every year. Buy the more permanent product, such as a Zippo lighter, and you will save money and keep down waste.

Buy whatever you can in bulk and pay attention to the kind of packaging a product has. Some estimates point to the fact that 50% of waste is packaging related.

Look for recycled paper products at the grocery store. They are usually cheaper than other products and quite often provide the same quality as the name-brand items. You can find facial tissue, toilet paper, napkins, paper plates, and other products that have been recycled.

If you change the oil in your car or lawn mower, take it to a local recycling center. Studies say that 2.1 million gallons of oil seep into our rivers and streams in a year's time. A quart of motor oil can contaminate over 250,000 gallons of drinking water. Call local gas stations or your energy board to find out the best places to recycle used motor oil.

The U.S. Postal Service estimates that every family in America receives over 300 pieces of junk mail every year. When you order anything through the mail, include a note that asks to not be included on any mailing lists that they may rent out. Most companies will oblige. This will dramatically cut down on your junk mail.

Use only biodegradable detergents and soaps. Also, you can use less of these products than is recommended by the manufacturer. They usually tell you to use more than is needed (for obvious reasons).

Plastic is one of the biggest polluters in our environment. Try to buy as little plastic as possible. Not only does it not decompose, but most things that are made from plastic can break easily and end up in the trash pile quickly. Toys are a good example of this. Opt for more heavy-duty toys such as blocks, wood cars and trucks, and hand-crafted items. These will be in the family for a long time.

Of course, the most practical items to recycle are paper products. Have a special box or container around the house for newspaper, junk mail, and other paper products. Also, a container for aluminum cans should be used.

The Time's the Cheapest

Everyone knows that long-distance rates vary depending on the day of the week and time of day. It is important that you know the rules for whatever long-distance company you use and also the guidelines for your local phone company. Some local companies around the country charge access fees, depending on the most active time of the day. If you don't know the rules the different companies enforce, make an effort to call in the next few days and find out. It could save you quite a bit of money if you know the cheapest times to call and make an effort to make long-distance calls at just those times.

Telephone Leases

Don't ever lease a telephone from the local telephone company. Telephone companies make oodles of money off these residential lease programs. Purchase your phones rather than renting them. The initial purchase of the equipment may cost you, but you will spend much less in the long run, since you won't be paying for the phone for years. Also, you walk away with the phone when you move as opposed to nothing. Buy good quality phones, so you won't have to be concerned about them breaking. If you check in the phone book, there should be a store in your area that sells reconditioned phones at about half off retail. Most of the time, the phone company will lease you reconditioned equipment anyway.

Household Message Center

If you want to save time and money at home, it's a great idea to establish a message center. Get a small bulletin board and plenty of thumbtacks. Put the bulletin board in a central area in the house and have all notes, messages, and lists attached to it. Make the family aware that any kind of communication should be tacked to this board. It can be especially helpful if you are like me and have ten messages and notes strewn all over the house. Also, a message center can be great for grocery lists and reminders to yourself.

Quick Call

Doesn't it annoy you that to get a number for someone in another state you have to call directory assistance, get their area code, then make a long-distance phone call just to get their complete number?

Here's the solution. Call 1-800-CALL-INFO to get around this hassle. You can get the number of anyone in the country with just their name and the city they live in. You can also get another number, plus they can automatically connect you. It costs about 75 cents per call. This is a savings when you consider that you will probably be charged for your local directory assistance and also a long-distance charge if you go the conventional route. I figure you could probably save as much as 50 cents per call and also a lot of hassle.

Another phone tip to keep in mind: If you find yourself on perpetual hold with electronic push-button-operated answering machines (you know, the kind that your credit card company has), try a new strategy. When they ask you to press 1 if you have a touch-tone phone, don't press a thing. Hold the line until someone comes on. Since most of us have touch-tone phones, the odds of you getting in through a rotary-phone option are far better.

Cellular Scams

If you have a cellular phone, beware of the latest scam. Criminals are tapping into radio frequencies and eavesdropping on phone calls. If they listen long enough they can get credit card information, business information, and bank account numbers. Be careful about what you talk about on cellulars, because they are not as secure as your phone at home. Also, your cordless phone at home can be an easy target since it also uses radio waves. Never discuss any confidential matters that you know could be used to someone else's advantage on these unsecured lines of communication. Especially, never give out bank account numbers or credit card numbers.

Writing Basics

Next time you want to make a long-distance phone call, think about writing a note instead. People love to receive letters in the mail, so it's much more special. If you're lucky, you'll get a reply back. If you want to be creative, send video or audio tapes with instructions to have the other party tape over them and send the tape back. Have everyone in the family pitch in their two cents worth. These ways of communicating are different and they will cost less in the long run.

Zap the Pests—Cheap

Most exterminators use a product that is called Durasband to get rid of almost all your household insects. Go to the local hardware or discount home supply store and purchase a bottle of Durasband and a regular garden sprayer. Mix according to directions and spray all along the outside of your house and in your basement, once in the spring and once in the fall. You can also use this spray indoors, but do so sparingly. Also, get two or three bottles of insect fogger and set those off twice a year in select parts of your home. If you do these two things, you will get just as good a job as the exterminator for about a quarter of the cost. If you are unfortunate enough to have fleas, you may need to repeat this process for several weeks. Keep an eye out for any major problems like carpenter ants or termites. If you do find these nasty critters, call in the pros.

The Painter's Friend

Doing your own painting around the house can save you a heap of cash because hiring a paint contractor can be costly. Do-it-yourself painting can be pretty easy and also rewarding when the job is done. With a little coaching, you can tackle walls, ceilings, woodwork, and even the exterior of your home.

The first thing you need to know to get started is that your equipment needs to be good. Nothing can make a job go slower and cut down on the quality of the work as much as poor equipment. Go to a reputable paint supplier and spend a little money on good quality scrapers, brushes, rollers, and ladders. You may spend a little more, but you will be able to use this equipment over and over in the years to come. Don't skimp. Remember that you are saving a lot by not hiring a professional painter.

Some exterior painting jobs don't need painting at all. Check the surface of your home by putting a little water on an area that looks bad and then rubbing it. If dirt comes off and not paint, you can probably make the house look brand-new again simply by cleaning it. For about $40 you can rent a power washer at a local rental store and clean the whole house in about half a day. Some power washers even come with special attachments to add bleach or detergent to do a perfect job. The cost of this power washer is significantly less than paying hundreds to paint the house yourself or hiring a contractor. Sometimes just power washing can prolong the life of the paint job. Obviously, if there is peeling paint and bare wood showing, this won't work. You'll need to repaint.

The cost of paint is escalating rapidly to the point that it's not uncommon to pay $30 for a gallon. Too rich for my blood. Call around to different paint stores and suppliers to find the best price. You don't want to go too cheap, though. Bad paint can be a bad investment, so make sure that what you are putting on will stay on. Latex is generally the best type of paint to use and is much easier to work with than oil-based paint. Soon, the government will ban all forms of oil-based paint, but it still has its uses for exterior priming and for interior woodwork.

The most important part of any paint job is how you prepare the surfaces for painting. A great preparation job will ensure the paint's adhesion. Scrape any loose or peeling paint and repair any holes or cracks in the surfaces with spackling or caulk. Sand any areas that look shabby or seem like there might be a problem with adhesion. Any bare wood should be primed with an oil-based primer. The oil-based paint soaks into the wood. Latex doesn't bond to bare wood properly but will bond to the oil-based paint. After the preparation work, make sure the surface is clean.

The painting is the easy and fun part. Conserve paint by using a pail with a handle instead of painting out of the can. It will be much easier for you also. When painting indoors, paint one wall at a time, first cutting in around the corners with your brush and then rolling out the rest of the wall. This method will ensure an even look because you will be rolling over wet brush edges immediately. On the exterior, you can cut in the whole house and then go back and roll if you prefer. No one will be able to tell the difference between where you brushed and rolled on an exterior surface.

On new interior woodwork, it is a good idea to put a prime coat on and then two coats of oil base. Be especially careful if you tackle woodwork because the paint has a tendency to run. I also recommend that you put two coats of latex on interior walls because they usually get a lot of abuse.

If you choose to paint your home, make sure you have plenty of touch-up paint left over for the years to come. Once a year you should pull out the touch-up cans and go around the entire house. Your paint job will last years longer if you keep it in good shape with this annual chore.

If you decide to hire a professional because you think you just can't handle the job or don't have time, go with a reputable firm that has insurance and plenty of references. Most painters will negotiate on price if you feel the cost is too high. You may try swapping out some of the work that you will do yourself for a lower price on the bid. Make sure the contract specifies exactly what you will be doing.

Caulk that Works

Don't ever use cheap caulk on the interior or exterior of your home. A silicone or polyurethane caulk is always better than inexpensive latex caulks. Why? For the small extra price you pay, the quality is many times better. Silicone expands and contracts with the changes in weather, seals more tightly, and doesn't crack. All this can add up to big savings when the utility bill comes. So if you see a sale on latex caulk, forget it. Get the good stuff and save a lot more in the long run.

Outdoor Chore

Take time this spring to clean that grimy old patio furniture. You should really do this twice a year to keep the furniture in good shape and keep it from corroding. Use a strong cleaner because the dirt build-up on patio furniture is usually tough to get off. It's a good idea to put the furniture indoors for the winter if you have the space to store it. Along these same lines, if you have a deck, clean it off every few years with a deck renewer and protect it with a quality wood preservative. You will prolong the life of the deck by many years.

Clean It Right

There are a number of condensed organic cleaners on the market that can make cleaning easier and less expensive. These cleaners usually come in gallon jugs, and it is your responsibility to mix the appropriate portions for different cleaning jobs. The best products have a citrus base, and you simply mix them with water to your desire. I recommend buying 4 or 5 professional squirt bottles, labeling them, and mixing them for different cleaning jobs. One gallon of condensed cleaner can last a year or two and can handle any job around the house, including windows. It sure would be nice to be able to throw away those 20 bottles of brand-name cleaners I never use! Check your local warehouse club or discount store for the different condensed cleaners available.

Use just a tablespoon of dishwashing detergent in the machine rather than a cup or more that the machine holds. You will be amazed that your dishes get just as clean as before and you will save in the long run. This trick should also be used when you're washing clothes. I think you'll find that many products take a lot less of the stuff than recommended to get the job done. Why? It's common sense that the more we use, the more they sell. Some liquid cleaners are so potent that you can dilute them 50% with water and they will still do the job. Try using less glass cleaner, dishwashing liquid, furniture polish, etc.

Cheap and Unique Cleaners

If you need cleaning supplies and are a little low on cash or run out of a certain type of cleaner, use some of these inexpensive alternatives: Shampoo will remove ring around the collar. Vinegar or lemon juice will cut grease and are also effective glass cleaners. When added to hot water, vinegar and lemon juice can also cut through clogged drains. If you freeze them into ice cubes, they can clean a garbage disposal. Use crumpled newspaper to clean mirrors and windows (no smudges). Hair spray will get out ink stains on shirts. Hydrogen peroxide works well on blood stains.

Kitchen Scrub

To prevent bacteria in your kitchen on counters, stoves, and in the refrigerator, use different sponges and towels for different duties such as wiping counters, cleaning dishes and drying dishes. Buy a value pack of sponges and use new ones every month or so. Clean your can opener every time you use it so you don't get rotten food build-up on the blade. Be careful to not use the same knives and cutting boards for vegetables and meats. Thaw frozen food in the refrigerator or in the microwave. Thawing food on the counter all day can be risky. Last, don't overcrowd your refrigerator because it will cost more to operate. Also, clean it out every couple of months.

Boarder Savings

Do you have an extra room in the house, or perhaps a finished basement that no one ever uses? Consider taking on a boarder to help defray your mortgage costs. Post notices at local colleges or companies. An ad in the newspaper is good, but be prepared to interview a lot of people before you can find one that seems appropriate. You might also check with the personnel department of major corporations. Many times they are looking for places to house executives or new employees from out of town. If you can, install separate eating and bathing facilities for the tenant if you want to minimize them getting in your way. The extra expense can be well worth it.

Duct Tape Fix-Ups

I was in the bookstore a while back and spotted a book about the hundreds of ways that you can use duct tape to fix things around the house. It first struck me as a cute book about impractical ways to use the tape. I then opened it up and realized all the very good uses for this amazing glue-like stuff. I also remembered that there are probably three or four things in my house that are held together by this miracle tape. Some ideas: repair a leaky hose, mend broken wires, repair a slight leak in pipes, clamp items down for gluing, fix punctures in air mattresses, seal leaks in rubber boots, and of course mend an air duct (how ingenious). There are hundreds of inventive ways it can be used. One note of caution: Always buy good-quality duct tape for added durability. You will notice the good stuff has a lot of thread mesh.

Soda Scrub

Buy a six-pack of soda water and use it to clean spots or pet stains out of your carpet or upholstery. The reason I suggest a six-pack is because the soda works best when it has plenty of fizz. So be prepared to open a new bottle if you have to. Soda water works better than any other cleaner on carpets and upholstery and is a fraction of the cost compared to name-brand cleaners. If you can keep on top of the stains, you will save big bucks on costly professional steam cleaners, too.

Carpet Envy

How do you know if the carpet you are installing in your home is good quality? First, check the density. Closely packed yarns and tight backing make for carpets that wear a long time. Simply bend the carpet backward and see if a lot of backing is visible through the pile. If there is, it is probably not good quality. It is not a good idea to buy cheap carpeting for high-traffic areas since it has a tendency to mat down. Always buy good padding to go under the carpet to provide more comfort and help the carpet last longer. If cost is a problem, do not skimp on quality. You would be better off buying less carpet or putting lower quality carpeting in low-traffic areas.

Gurgled Money

Listerine was once the only over-the-counter mouthwash to fight plaque and gingivitis (inflammation of the gums) that carried the ADA seal of approval. Studies have shown that this product can reduce plaque buildup by about 22%, as well as give you fresher breath. Now, the private label firms supplying similar mouthwashes—like Wal-Mart and Kmart—also have the ADA seal. These brands cost about 50% less than the name-brand products. If you diligently brush and floss, you probably don't need mouthwash, anyway. Check with your dentist to see what is best for you.

Christmas Card Recycling

Oh, what to do with all the wonderful Christmas cards you received this year? Consider recycling. Cut off the backs of the cards and turn them into postcards for next Christmas. Make the cuts clean so there are no ragged edges. You will save money by not buying cards next year and save on postage. Mailing postcards is 30% cheaper than sending cards. You'll also save time, because the size of a postcard restricts those long stories about how the year has gone. A word of caution: Make a note of who gave you which card so you don't send the same card to the person who sent it to you in the first place. How embarrassing!

Flower Power

Make flowers last much longer by following these steps:

1. Cut off the stems one half inch from the bottom. Cut at an angle so the stem does not choke against the bottom of the vase.

2. Make a tiny incision on the stem near the base of the bloom. This allows the stem to "breathe" and release water build-up.

3. Fill a clean vase with fresh water (spring water is best).

4. Add a natural preservative made of two squeezes of lemon juice, a teaspoon of sugar, and a few drops of club soda.

5. Change the water every few days.

6. Keep your flowers out of direct sunlight and away from heater vents.

Follow these tips and double the life of your flowers.

Home-Based Business Basics

There are definite advantages to running your own business at home, whether part-time or full-time. If you have a hobby or trade that you feel you are good at, it is a good idea to use this skill to your advantage by starting small and building the business as much as possible. You can positively affect your tax position by using a business to deduct items you would regularly buy anyway, and you may be able to generate a substantial income for yourself. Most people are coming to realize that having your own business is about the only way to get wealthy anymore.

There is really no perfect time to start a business, and you really can't predict if it will be a success. The energy, vision, and skills you bring to the table are the determining factors. Here are some important things to keep in mind if you want to launch a new business:

Do a tremendous amount of research and work in advance. Talk to people who are in the industry you are looking to get into, and ask lots of questions. Spend time at the library reading and researching. If you decide to go ahead with your business launch, do a lot of the legwork well before your actual launch, such as opening up bank accounts, preparing a business plan, filing for a business license, and setting up your books. This will free up time to generate income when you launch. You shouldn't have to worry about small details then.

The worst time to start a new business is when your life is in turmoil. Ironically, this is when most people think it is the best time because they see it as a change. If you experience a family breakup or some big emotional letdown, wait until you have worked it out before you take on the risk of starting your own business.

To start, begin your business on a part-time basis at home. Quite often, this isn't possible, but if the circumstances allow it, you can test the waters before you quit your present job. This is why it's a great idea to start a business that is related to a hobby or trade you are familiar with. If you know the territory, it may be easier to start part-time and then expand from there.

Be a $ensible $aver about spending money at first. You don't need to go out and hire management consultants or market researchers when you can do these types of things yourself. The biggest thing that takes most businesses down is lack of capital. While it's true that it takes money to make money, the new business owner has to be smart and creative with cash. Often, when a business is small and under-capitalized, the best money decisions are made because they mean life and death for the company. As the company generates more capital, owners tend to throw money at problems, rather than trying to creatively solve them with the least amount of capital. It is vital that you spend money on a good lawyer and accountant, though. They will save you lots of money in the long run.

Be prepared for the ups and downs in your business. Every business experiences failures, but it is with these failures that the company grows. A slow quarter or even a slow year is not uncommon. You need to stick with it for as long as possible to see good results. If your business shows little sign of growth after two years, it's probably time to reevaluate your business choice.

Make sure the product or service you are promoting has compelling advantages to other competing products in the industry. Just because someone is selling the same thing you are and making a killing, does not mean you will automatically make money, too. Don't wait for business to come to you because it never does. You have to go out and show the advantages of your product over others.

Also, don't automatically assume you can get a business loan from a bank. Banks don't like to lend to start-up businesses without sufficient collateral. You'll probably have to invest your savings, borrow against your home, borrow from family or friends, or tap a partner's capital.

Starting Small for Big Tax Breaks

A great way to get plenty of tax deductions is to start your own small business either full- or part-time. If you have your own business you may be entitled to a wide range of deductions to offset your business income.

Any expense related to the running of that business can be deductible. This can include advertising, bank charges, bad debts, office and utility expenses, etc. There are actually 18 different categories as well as "other expenses." In addition, you can deduct the cost of inventory that is resold by your business.

You can also deduct interest expenses if you borrow money to finance the operation of your company. You may also deduct the cost of equipment through the "Section 179" provision.

Here are some other things that you may already own that can be tax deductible depending on the business you go into:

- Autos
- Auto expenses
- Home
- Computers
- Travel
- Books and subscriptions
- Calculators, typewriter, and recorders
- Education expenses

All these tax advantages can make it much easier to venture out and open your own business. One of the best things to do is run your business from a spare room in your home. You can deduct the percentage of space used on your taxes. That would include a percentage of your mortgage and utilities. The percentage of space in your home must be used exclusively for your business, though.

If there is a hobby you have or a skill that can make you money, go for it. You don't have to risk your livelihood. You can start working in the evening or weekends and see if you can turn it into a full-time profit maker. If it is something you enjoy, you will most likely make money, and the sense of accomplishment will be tremendous.

Independent Woes

Think twice about being hired as an independent contractor for a company. A positive is that you can take deductions that an employee can't, but there are negatives you may not be seeing. First, as an independent contractor, you will automatically pay both your portion and what an employee pays for Social Security tax, which will double your FICA tax liability. Second, depending on the company, you may be missing out on thousands of dollars worth of benefits such as health and disability insurance. I am not saying that you should not be an independent contractor, but you should compare the financial aspects of being an employee. You may find that employee status is more advantageous.

How to Stretch Your Paycheck

The obvious source that provides an opportunity for you to live a more comfortable life is your paycheck. Most people overlook simple ways to structure their paychecks to get the biggest bang for their bucks. Think of your household income as the sales of your family "company." Like any kind of sales revenue, your income needs some analysis to find hidden opportunities for improvement.

When reviewing your income, start with your gross salary before deductions, not your net paycheck. Looking at your paycheck stubs, consider some of the following important points:

- Are you withholding too much in taxes? The truth is the majority of Americans withhold much more than is needed. You should adjust your deductions according to how much you think you will deduct at the end of the year. You should be able to come up with a rough idea of this figure. Are you going to take an IRA, medical, or mortgage deduction? If you plan to take all or any of these deductions, you should calculate them into your allowable withholding. There is no use in loaning Uncle Sam the money when you could be earning interest off it for one year.

- Do you really need all the insurance you are paying for through payroll deductions? Most paycheck stubs are littered with unnecessary insurance deductions. You may be able to get the insurance cheaper someplace else, or at least have a trusted insurance agent check out your employee coverage. Your spouse may have duplicate coverage you are paying extra to provide. If you check these things out and find areas of improvement, you can put an extra $50–$100 per month into your pocket.

- You may be over-withholding on FICA if you changed jobs this year. Employers are required to start withholding all over again when you start a new job, but the most they can base their withholding on is $37,000. If you have been earning $40,000 for most of the year and you switch to a job paying $45,000, then you need to make sure you are not paying too much FICA tax. You will get it back when you file your return, but why wait? If you get that money immediately, put it to work in a good investment plan. Keep in mind that you can't stop FICA withholding no matter what you do, but you can claim additional allowances and reduce your withholding by visiting your company's personnel department. Your take-home pay will be more by the next week.

- Take complete advantage of any company-sponsored retirement plans. These plans are a great way to reduce your tax burden and help you start a savings program for the future.

- Are you due a raise? If it's been a couple of years since the boss has given you a raise, now is a good time to ask. If your company is stingy with a buck and is not paying you what you could get elsewhere, look at finding another job. This is really the best way for you to get a significant raise.

- Try borrowing from your company's 401(K) plan or your credit union if you need money. The rates are usually more favorable than a bank's, and you have the advantage of dealing with your own company rather than some unknown banker.

A careful review of your paycheck with either your company's personnel department or your office manager is a good idea. It may alert you to some company benefits you may have overlooked or forgotten about in the past few years. You may also find you are withholding too much. Keep a watchful eye on your paycheck at least twice a year to make sure you are maximizing its benefits.

Fax It

You might consider using your fax machine more often to send notes or correspondence, especially if you do a lot of long-distance calling. Faxing cuts down on wasted money and time spent on unnecessary small talk. To save even more, send your faxes late at night when the rates are cheaper. A faxed one-page letter can cost even less than sending a letter through the mail. Of course, any faxes that you send locally are totally free! I am starting to use my fax machine more and I have noticed it's very efficient.

ACTION LIST

1. Been a while since you had your furnace and air conditioner checked out? Call a reputable professional and have them do a routine checkup on your systems.

    Date completed: _____

2. If you have a lot of junk laying around the house, consider having a garage sale either alone or with your neighbors. This is a great way to pick up some extra cash.

    Date completed: _____

3. Consider painting your home yourself if it is need of a face-lift. It is not difficult to learn how to paint and you can save hundreds off the cost of hiring a professional.

    Date completed: _____

4. If you are in need of extra money and have a hobby or craft you are good at, consider making it a part-time business. A home-based business can generate lots of income and also plenty of tax deductions.

    Date completed: _____

CHAPTER 10

Having Fun for Much Less

> With money in your pocket, you are wise and you are handsome, and you sing well too.
>
> —Yiddish proverb

We all like to have fun, but the cost of entertaining ourselves is going up every year. Between going to the movies, eating out, seeing an occasional concert, and keeping up on our hobbies, etc., the average American family spends about $3,500 per year. Unfortunately, this is about 20 times the amount we give to charities!

It's easy to see why we spend so much. If you take the family out to the movies, you can rack up a bill of $30 to $40 including tickets and the junk food. If you and your spouse or significant other go to a restaurant, have a few glasses of wine and then go out dancing, you'll probably get at least a $75 tab. This doesn't even include the cost of the babysitter. If you take the whole gang to the ballpark, between tickets, parking, and refreshments, you'll be doing well to get by with $100 for just a few hours of fun. Fun is expensive, but as with anything else, if you look in the right places you may have a better time and do it on the cheap as well.

Cheap Night Out

There is no such thing as a cheap night out on the town anymore. By the time you add up dinner, a few drinks, and a movie, a couple is looking at a cost of around $60. If you really want to go cheaply, invite a few friends over, have dinner, and watch a video. Next time, they will invite you to their humble abode and the night will be on them. You can even make it a game to see who can throw the cheapest VCR party. I think you'll find this type of evening much more relaxing and a better way to spend time with friends.

Potluck Surprise

Potluck dinner parties are becoming popular again. Why go to the enormous expense and hassle of throwing a lavish dinner party when you can invite three or four couples over and assign them different entrees? You can also assign someone to bring paper plates, napkins, and utensils. Since everyone is contributing, you will be left with less mess and more money in your pocketbook.

The $ensible $aver's Greatest Entertainment Spot

Libraries are fast becoming the hip place for savers to be. They're not just for books anymore. Libraries provide videotapes, cassette learning courses, compact discs, how-to manuals, and much more. You can learn a new language, travel to the ends of the earth, listen to the latest CD, cook with the great chefs, or learn how to fix that leaky faucet, all under one roof. The best part is that most of this is all free or very low priced. The next time you think about buying a book or tape, or renting a video, always think about the library first. You'll save a bundle. And, if you are single, it's not a bad place to meet people, either.

Lottery Losers

Face the fact that you are a loser if you buy a lottery ticket. Not a loser in general, but definitely a lottery loser. Don't even waste a buck on any one of these slick games. In a normal lottery (6 out of 54 numbers), you have a one in 12.5 million chance of winning. Put another way, your chances of winning that lottery are less than getting hit by lightning seven times in your lifetime! Do you think that will happen? "Somebody's always winning!" cry the promotional ads, but it won't be you no matter how many tickets you buy. Why do I mention this in the entertainment chapter? Because if you want to play for fun, go right ahead, but don't think you're going to win.

Second Time Around

To save on the cost of movies, don't see first-run movies. If you wait a couple of months, you can usually rent the same movie for only a few dollars. The whole family can see the flick for less than the cost of one first-run ticket. You can save a lot of money if you have a big family. Also, check your local library for video rentals; the library may rent them for free or as little as $1.

Coupon Books

Each year, purchase an Entertainment coupon book in your area. This book is a great way to get two-for-one offers throughout your city. If you go out of town, it might be a good idea to call the main office (Entertainmet Publications: 1-800-285-5525) and ask to purchase a coupon book for the selected city. You will find that on these vacations you will more than make up the cost of the books. In the back of the coupon book there are also coupons for cheap airfares and car rentals throughout the country. You can also usually purchase this book or a similar one at large department stores or through local charities.

Ball Park and Theater Knockout

I wondered how the $1 movie theater could make money on such cheap tickets. Then I saw the concession line! Don't ever buy soft drinks, candy, or food at the ball park or movie theater. You can easily spend the price of a ticket, and then some, on these items. I would love to own the concessions. Eat your fill before the event or bring along a snack for yourself and the kids. Most theaters and sporting events will let you bring in some light snacks in a satchel. Just don't bring a picnic basket.

Salad Madness

Take advantage of the current popularity of salad bars and buffets. You can eat all you want at very inexpensive prices. Many restaurants are starting to see that it's profitable to offer a lot of food in a buffet and charge a small amount. Seek out all-you-can-eat cafeterias and also look for salad-only joints that have good, low-fat items. Why should you pay six bucks for just one item on the menu when you can have anything you want for $4.99?

Dining Deals

If you like to eat out, like I do, use coupons and take advantage of special deals whenever possible. Many restaurants participate in advertising campaigns that offer you some sort of discount. The best offers are two for ones. A good offer is also a free meal or sandwich after you have purchased several. If you are planning a meal out for a birthday or anniversary, phone around and find out who offers any freebies. There are some restaurants that offer a complete meal for the special occasion.

St. Valentine the Saver

How about some ideas to cut your costs on Valentine's Day? I suppose the greatest idea to keep the cost down is doing something special rather than just buying the traditional items. Why not provide breakfast in bed, or tell your significant other that you will be their Valentine for the day. Anything that they want for that day will be fulfilled by you. Why not buy an inexpensive goody basket, or perhaps make a promise to stop doing something (like leaving off the toothpaste cap or leaving your clothing on the floor of the bedroom) that has been driving your partner batty? If you insist on getting roses, look for a discounted shop that sells a dozen for $15 rather than plunking down $50 or $60 for the same thing. Consider buying less expensive flowers such as carnations instead of roses. Spending more money doesn't necessarily make the gift more special.

Movies on the Cheap

Consider going to the dollar movies more often (actually, some of these theaters now charge $1.50). Most areas have some sort of discount theater that plays second-run movies. I usually wait four to five months for a movie that I really want to see to come out in the dollar theaters. I just can't get myself to pay $6 or more for a first-run movie. There's not much difference between the experience of the first-run theater and that of the second-run theater, other than possibly sound quality. Remember not to buy junk food from the concession stand, though. You will blow the "cheapness" of the whole experience. Bring some peanuts or candy from home and split a coke with your significant other.

The Smart Tipper

Whenever I go out to eat, I often don't know the best amount to tip the waiter or waitress. Being the $ensible $aver, I'm always looking for ways to keep the tips down, but you have to be courteous, too, since they all work hard for a living. Unfortunately, this is not true in some of the restaurants I've been in! I get very upset about bad service.

The following are some guidelines that the $ensible $aver should use when tipping in various places:

- Waiter/waitress: 15% of the bill, before tax. Add another 3% to 5% if service is outstanding. Giving less of a tip doesn't make the waiter or waitress do a better job the next time; they'll only think you are cheap.

- Captain: 5% of bill. Specify that you want this money to go to the captain or else the restaurant will give the whole tip to the waiter.

- Hostess or headwaiter at a quality restaurant: If you want the best seats, tip them $5–$10 in cash when you walk in the door.

- Bartender: 50 cents per drink or 15% of the total check.

- Restroom attendant, hat check, or doorman: 50 cents

- Nightclubs: Valet parking, $1 to $2.

- Hotels: Valet, room service, or bartender should all receive a minimum of $1. Bellman: 50 cents to $1 per bag...this goes for skycaps at airports, also.

- Sports arenas, concerts and race tracks: A $5–$10 tip should get you some unused reserved seats that may be better than the original ones you had.

Casino Strategy

Although I don't advocate gambling, I realize that a large percentage of Americans play the lottery and also go to the blackjack table every once in a while. That's okay, as long as you see it as a way to have fun and not as a way to make money. We all gamble enough in our lives just by living them day to day. Let's not add insult to injury by taking hundreds of dollars a year and blowing it at the casino or in the lottery line.

If you want to gamble, take a very small amount of money—an amount you are willing to lose. The best way to look at the situation is ask yourself, "How much is this entertainment worth to me?" Be honest with yourself. If you win 50% more than you started with, take your original bet and 50% of your winning and stash them away. Do whatever you can to avoid dipping into your original bet. If you don't do this, you may lose your money fast and want to head for the ATM. By following the 50% rule, you will not be tempted to spend over your limit.

Government Fun

Flip through the government pages of your local White Pages and you will be surprised at what you will find. They are full of resources and facilities for your amusement and fun. Under city listings, you may find zoos, golf courses, swimming pools, recreation centers, parks, aquariums, dance halls, libraries, theaters, boat-ing centers, and art museums. Under county listings, look for libraries, parks, and educational services. State listings generally include parks. Under public schools, you will find a wide range of departments at local colleges and universities. Call the numbers that interest you and ask to be placed on their mailing list of upcoming events. Most activities and events are free or low-cost.

Having Fun and Saving Money

Do not base how much fun you have on the amount of money you spend. Look for activities that are inexpensive and enjoyable for you and your family. Here are 35 ways to have a great time without digging too deeply into your pocket:

- Visit the local zoo and feed the monkeys.

- Go to a free concert in the park.

- Pack a picnic lunch and drive to an out-of-the-way spot.
- Window-shop at your favorite stores.
- Eat early-bird specials at local restaurants. Then go home and watch a good movie on TV.
- Dress up and enjoy a special dinner at home, complete with wine and candles.
- Go hiking or camping.
- Go gallery hopping. See the latest art exhibits.
- Go to your public library and hang out in your favorite section. Catch up on reading you've been putting off.
- Take a drive in the country and enjoy the scenery. Stop at local stores and restaurants to taste a different flavor of life.
- Visit friends in a nearby city (plan to arrive around lunchtime for those of you who are obsessive cheapies).
- Eat dinner at home. Then go out for dessert and coffee.
- Seek out restaurants that that offer great lunch specials. Avoid eating out for dinner if possible.
- Use two-for-one coupons when dining out.
- Go to free lectures and seminars offered by local museums.
- Invite friends over for a video and some cards. Have everyone bring a favorite dish.
- Take an afternoon stroll with a good friend.
- Have a beer and pizza party for friends, rather than a high falootin' dinner party.
- Whip out the old Monopoly and Trivial Pursuit games.
- Learn to paint, sculpt, or do some sort of craft.
- Find a field near the airport to lie under the paths of incoming planes, and listen to your heart race.
- Be a do-it-yourselfer around the house.
- Teach yourself aerobics.
- Get involved in a local political club.
- Play poker with friends for penny stakes.
- Learn to be a great cook.

- Go to the dog track or the casino and place only $2 bets. Don't break this rule, and you better not gamble long.

- Go to places in the city you have never been to see the sights.

- Get involved with your local church.

- Learn a foreign language through tapes.

- Join a choral group or try out for a play.

- Watch a high school football or basketball game.

- Buy books at discount warehouses.

- Play nine holes of golf at a public course. Use public courts to play a set or two of tennis.

- Spend special time with your family just talking about the events of the day.

ACTION LIST:

1. Take the family out for a night at the dollar movies rather than the first-run movies.

    Date completed: _____

2. Next time you think about meeting friends out at a local night spot, invite them over for popcorn and a movie instead.

    Date completed: _____

3. Visit your local library and take an informal tour. You may be pleasantly surprised by the services they provide.

    Date completed: _____

4. Purchase an Entertainment coupon book to save 50% on dining out.

    Date completed: _____

CHAPTER 11

Traveling Made Easy and Cheap

Do not rely on your present good fortune; prepare for the year when it may leave you.

—Chinese Proverb

Doesn't everyone need a good vacation? The problem is it takes "mucho dinero" to make it happen. If you are looking for good accomodations, airfares, or fabulous vacation spots, you may just end up mortgaging the house to get them.

One night's stay in a better hotel can cost as much as $200 per night. The so-called bargain motels can be $50 or more. If you want to visit Disney World, you can pay as much as $500 per day just to entertain the whole family. Walt would turn over in his grave if he knew how difficult it was for the average American to visit his wonderland. Likewise, if you aren't smart, you can get really burned by overpriced tour promotions.

But there is a way you can have your vacation without having to pay a fortune. If you know how to get the best rates on airfare, lodging, and entertainment when traveling, you will be able to cut hundreds of dollars off your vacation costs without affecting the quality of your trip.

Travel Agent Jitters

If you use a travel agent to book your vacations, it never hurts to do a little back-up checking to make sure they are getting you the best rates. Call a few of the airlines yourself to check for the lowest fares. If you are traveling on a package deal, call the company yourself and ask questions your travel agent might have overlooked. My experience has been that most travel agents don't do exhaustive background work to make sure that they get you the best possible deal. The only way they make money is to help as many clients as possible, which means they have less time to spend finding the best deal for each client. Always do investigative work yourself to make sure you are getting the best deal possible.

Can a Travel Agent Really Help?

There's talk that travel agents might start charging fees to issue airline tickets, their main source of commission income. If this becomes reality, I think there will be a lot of consumers wondering if they really need a travel agent's services. As it stands now, travel agents can be a good bargain if you find the right one, but there are some things you should watch out for if you choose to use their services all the time.

First, travel agents don't necessarily always have access to the lowest fares, like they say they do. They can save you lots of time by instantly looking up the available fares on their computer, but most of the time they don't have instant access to charter flights or special promotional rates. To find these rates, it takes some legwork, and most agents do not have the time or inclination to find these rates. It's not that they don't know about them. Usually the commissions are too low on airline tickets to make it worth the extra time the agents have to put in.

Likewise, some large travel companies get special deals from certain airlines if they sell a large amount of tickets. This can make your agent biased toward an airline on any given day. You may have to pay a little more if they steer you toward this airline. To check to see if you are getting the lowest rates, simply do some homework by occasionally checking airline rates yourself. Metropolitan newspapers have the lowest rates for the week in their weekend editions. This can be an excellent guide. But never substitute your ability to do some research yourself.

Travel agents can sometimes get you good rates on hotels, but the best route for you is to become a member of one of the many discount travel clubs and coupon books in the country. The Entertainment book (Entertainment Publications: 1-800-285-5525) is a great choice. It offers a 50% discount on hotels throughout the world. I have used this service several times and saved a bundle.

The one area a travel agent can really help you in is booking a room, rental car, or airline ticket when the tickets are sold out. How do they do this? Many large agencies have the ability to access what is called "blocked space." This is space set aside by a hotel or airline that is made available for cancellations and last-minute emergencies. An agent can have access to this space when normal travelers can't. Agencies can also use their clout to book car rentals even though there are no special programs available to them.

Another way agents can help tremendously is if a flight is canceled or you are bumped. They have immediate access to computers that can instantly find you an alternative route. If you ever have an airline problem, it's best to call your agent rather than waiting in line at the airport with 50 other people.

Don't think that you can hand over all the details of your special tour or vacation to a travel agent. Be prepared to follow up on many details yourself so that you know what's going on before you leave. Even though I often use a travel agent, I like to do a lot of the planning myself. I save lots of money this way and I always feel confident when I walk out the door of my home headed for some faraway place. Overall, you should use a travel agent to help you plan most excursions, but don't take their advice as gospel.

Cruisin' to $ensible $avings

If you're planning a vacation, you should consider a four- or seven-day cruise. There has never been a better time to get a deal on a good cruise because many cruise lines are offering cut rates to compete in the market.

Another great reason to take a cruise is because of the unique treatment you'll receive onboard. On almost all cruise ships, food and service are top priorities, meaning you get three gourmet meals a day with luxurious snacks in between. A steward will clean your room twice a day, and if you need room service, someone is there in a flash. To get this level of service on a normal ground excursion, you'd have to pay a bundle. But since it's all included in a cruise package, it's very affordable. You'll be treated like a king on a court jester's budget.

You'll also be able to relax on a cruise more than on other trips. You have the choice of just sitting around and doing nothing or taking part in ship activities and shore excursions.

Here are some tips on the easy ways to book the most inexpensive cruise:

1. Book your cruise a year in advance. If you book early, the cruise line is just beginning to fill the boat so it will give great rates to get booking off to a good start. If you book a year early, buy in at about three levels below the category of cabin you want. Usually, people who book this far in advance get bumped up three or four categories since cruise lines tend to sell so many cheaper cabins. Overall, this is the best time to book.

2. If you can't book early, wait until about two months before the cruise when the cruise line is trying to make sure it fills the ship before sailing. If you do book at this time, make sure you buy the cabin you want since it will be harder to get bumped up.

3. Ask your travel agent lots of questions about the different lines. For example, if you're looking for a quiet boat, say so. You don't want to be put on a Spring Break cruise.

4. If you have a choice of a late or early dinner seating on the cruise, pick the late seating. The late seating is usually followed by the evening entertainment, so you don't have a lot of lag time between eating and fun.

5. Call The Cruise Line (1-800-327-3021), based in Miami, Florida, for discounted fares on cruises around the world. The company will send you its cruise magazine with all the latest deals. The Cruise Line also has spur-of-the-moment cruises that are exceptional values.

With some advance planning, you can take a seven-day cruise to the Caribbean for $1,000–$1,200 per person or take a four-day cruise to the Bahamas for around $500 per person. Bon voyage!

Pay Phone Heist

Watch out for pay phones in airports. You will pay up to five times as much as you normally do if you get a pay phone that pays hefty commissions to the establishment where it is installed. If you dial person-to-person, you'll really get stung. To avoid these traps, always carry a calling card from your long-distance carrier. All you have to do is punch in your direct access code to be charged regular rates.

High-Flying Scams

Never pay an extra fee for plane travel insurance. It's just very high-priced life insurance. Airports are notorious for machines that shoot out "$100,000 worth of accidental death and dismemberment insurance for only $8.99." It sounds great, but the policies usually cover you for only one trip. The odds are in the multi-millions that you will be in an accident and collect on the insurance. If your dependents need protection, you should already have plenty of life insurance that covers you in all instances, not just a plane crash.

Take the A-Train

Since the price of flying continues to go up, consider taking the train next time you travel. Admittedly, Amtrak isn't exactly The Orient Express, but for shorter distances it's fine. When you add the time it takes to get to and from the airport, and layover hours, train travel can be quite appealing. Another advantage to train travel is that you get to see the scenery on some very unique routes. Also, your seats are much bigger on the train. It's a shame that America doesn't have the train service that Europeans have, but what we have is adequate and inexpensive for short hauls.

Should You Use a Ticket Consolidator?

Beware of travel agencies that claim to be "ticket consolidators," which operate by buying tickets in bulk and passing along the savings. In reality, for domestic flights the savings are very small and many of these consolidators still charge more than the lowest fare available. Also, some consolidators don't accept credit cards. This will leave you exposed if there are any disputes. Your best bet is to find a respected travel agent who you know will work hard to find you the cheapest fares. You can also do some investigative work yourself by calling the airlines that depart from your area.

Crazy Vacation Homes

Boy, it sure would be nice to have a vacation home. It sure would be dumb, also. Vacation homes are rarely a good investment despite what vacation area realtors might say. These homes or condominiums usually cost a ton of money to buy and maintain, and that giant sucking sound (as Ross Perot would say) continues on, year after year. In almost all cases the rental income received never helps to "pay for" the investment. You have to consider the risk factor associated with real estate investments. As soon as a recession hits, vacation properties are often the first investments to drop in value.

Frequent Flyer Dilemma

The IRS has had a strong position for many years that frequent flyer miles paid for by a company but used by an employee should be considered income to the employee. Fortunately, up to this point, Congress has not acted on these beliefs. This may be changing. The IRS has been auditing frequent fliers and imposing income taxes on individuals who sell their frequent flyer miles. This could be an indicator that sooner or later all frequent flyer miles will be taxed. In the meantime, the IRS is likely to do more investigations toward making you pay some taxes on your frequent flyer miles.

Satellite Savvy

Consider leaving your car in satellite parking at airports rather than parking by the terminal. You will generally have to take a shuttle to your terminal, but the cost savings is great. Also, many cities have bus services that will take you to the airport for less than you would pay for parking. The advantage to this is you can generally park your car in a safer area, or even at home if the bus stop is close. Of course, if it's convenient, the best route to go is having someone take you to the airport and then pick you up.

Travel Promotions that Really Hurt

Even though law enforcement agencies around the country have been beefing up prosecution of travel agency scams, deceptive promotional travel deals are still being heavily marketed. These promotions generally try to make you think you've just won the lottery but they turn out to be very deceptive and mostly scams.

The people running these operations are pros at the con. An example of one of these scams may go something like this: You receive a gold-leafed certificate in the mail that entitles you to a week's vacation at an exotic resort for only $199. These documents look official. The sales material is so compelling. Many people "check it out," even though it seems too good to be true. You call the company, which explains the offer and even gives you references. Once you call the references (people or companies in on the scam), you are sold. You call back and purchase the "deluxe" package for only $399 because it's a much better deal.

The reality is that you have just given your credit card number to a company you know nothing about, and now it has carte blanche to bill you for almost anything. You may get to go on the trip, but in the process, you'll be subjected to a high-pressure sales pitch for a time-share property. You may not even get all the benefits of the vacation if you don't buy the time-share. These types of scams are very common.

You may be told that you could have gotten the "special" price, but unfortunately those dates are sold out because of the spectacular offer and because you didn't call soon enough. If you would like to, though, you can upgrade to a "premium" package and still get a great deal. The gimmick here is that the price of the upgrade more than covers the cost of the vacation for the promoter.

Still, the more slimy operators will just take your money, close up shop, and move on to the next state to scam someone else.

The latest certificate scam involves promoters using the logos of famous and respected travel companies, hotels, and tour operators. They may have paid to get the rights to use the logos but the offer has nothing to do with the bigger companies. The big-name companies many times have little control over how their names are used. This is all in an effort to add credibility to the ridiculous offer.

Promoters have adopted two new tactics to get around the fraud regulations. First, the certificates they send out no longer say you've "won" a vacation. Instead they say that you "will receive" a trip. What you find out later is that to get the trip, you have to pay for it.

Secondly, you'll probably see some testimonials from former travelers. These might be legitimate, which means it's harder for regulatory agencies to get them. These testimonials simply show satisfied customers. Don't be fooled by these testimonials, though; they are often set-ups.

Whatever the scam, and I'm sure there are others I've missed, the best place for any mail of this nature is in the trash can with the rest of the junk mail.

Bumped Up and Out

Want to get free plane fares? Next time you schedule an airline flight, ask if the flight is almost full. If it is, book your seat. When it comes time to fly, arrive half an hour early and tell the ticketing agent that you would be willing to volunteer to be bumped onto a later flight if the plane is over-booked. If the plane ends up being too crowded, you will be the first one asked to be bumped.

The result will be the airline booking you on a later flight and a free plane ticket for the next time you fly! If you have to stay overnight, the airline will usually pay for your hotel and food (within reason).

The only catch is that you have to have the time to spare. You might want to try this only on a leisurely trip. This doesn't work all the time, so be patient. Remember, the airline doesn't want to give out free tickets, so it often happens that they are able to squeeze all the passengers in at the last minute.

Forego 800 Numbers

It's not always the best idea to call larger hotel companies' 800 numbers when you want to book a room at the best price. Since hotel room rates change constantly, even several times during a single day, the toll-free operators may not have the latest rates. It's best to call the hotel directly to make sure you get the newest and lowest rate. Believe me, it's well worth the dollar you may pay making a long-distance telephone call. Don't forget to mention any clubs that you may belong to that offer special discounts. If you ask, you can usually get the hotel corporate rate that can save you as much as 10% off the regular rates.

Travel Credit

When traveling, try to use your credit card as much as possible. Most card companies have special departments to help you if your card is stolen or lost. Also, the card issuers will do everything in their power to resolve difficult situations with vendors. If you pay with cash, you are just plain out of luck. If you are going out of the country, definitely use your credit card. Due to wholesale exchange rates, card companies get better rates than you can. These rates are usually passed on to the cardholder. Again, using your card gives you added protection, especially if you purchase out of the country. Finally, always book vacation packages, rental cars, and hotels on your card.

Travel Agency Insurance

Always buy travel insurance through your travel agent rather than a tour operator. The reason is simple: If you buy from the tour operator and the operator goes bankrupt, which has happened several times recently, your policy will be worthless and your money will be gone. When you buy a policy through your travel agency, the agency usually uses an outside insurance company, which often is very stable and reliable. Even if the travel agent goes under, the insurance company will still pay off because they are independently owned. When you do purchase these policies, check for any exclusionary clauses that would increase your liability or seem unfair. Ask lots of questions. Also, when you book tours through any company, make sure the company belongs to a national consumer protection company, which can help you if there is any kind of dispute.

Hotel Calling

When you have more than one call to make from a hotel or pay phone and you are using a calling card, don't hang up after each call. Simply push the # button to stay connected to your current long-distance carrier. By doing this, you will avoid being charged for another call. Most hotel computers cannot decipher this way of calling as more than one call. Try it; it works.

These Prices Are Headed Higher

We will see a lot of rate increases in the travel industry. Auto rental rates will probably rise about 10% over the next year or so. Hotel rooms will rise by about 4%, and travel costs abroad will go up substantially by about 20%, especially in Europe. Look for special discounts on cruises, because this market is very competitive. A cruise is probably the best travel deal out there.

Rely Only on Yourself

To get the best deal on a cruise vacation, don't rely totally on your travel agent. Not all of them are knowledgeable about cruises, and some promote only a few cruise lines. Check the most recent issues of *Travel Weekly*, which are available at your local library. Some issues have specific cruise guides that can help you pinpoint the best cruise for you. Then you can ask agents about these cruises. Get prices from many different agents. Prices vary from agent to agent. Your best bet is to go to a cruise-only agent and ask them about any special deals they may be offering. These agencies can usually get the best deals because they buy cruise cabins in bulk and then resell them. Ask them about cash rebates, free airfare to the departure port, flat rates for inside and outside cabins, free passage for a third and fourth passenger, and free cabin upgrades. As a final measure, you might check with the cruise company itself, which may have an even better price.

Foreign Cash

If you are planning a trip out of the country, you should get some of the foreign country's currency before you leave. Call your local bank, which either has the currency or can help you get it. Once you enter the other country, you may not be able to cash a traveler's check right away and you will usually need money fast to pay for hotels, food, and cabs. Also, exchange rates are horrendous at foreign airports, so this will allow you to have a little cash until you are able to get to a foreign bank where rates are much more reasonable. Rates are clearly posted and you should become familiar with them before you exchange.

Super-Saver Refunds

Most airlines do not allow refunds on tickets purchased as "super-savers." However, if you need to change your travel plans, don't assume this policy is absolute. A good travel agent can usually get you a refund within a few days or even a week after booking. When you buy your ticket through an agent, the reservation is made immediately, but the airline is often not paid for several days or a week. During this time, a good travel agent can cancel the reservation and get your money back. Of course, the agent is not required to do this because technically "super-savers" are non-refundable; however, if pressed hard enough or if you are a good customer, your agent may give you a refund. It is not in the airline's best interest to advertise these "exceptions," so make your travel agent aware you know it is possible.

Budget Motels that Deliver the Goods

There are over 500,000 budget motel rooms in the United States. Many budget motel chains offer the tired traveler a good room at a fair price. Here's a brief list of the biggest hotel chains in the country and a rundown of costs:

- Best Western is the world's largest company of independently owned motels with about 2,000 in the United States and another 1,500 in 49 other countries. Each property has a coffee shop or provides a continental breakfast; most have swimming pools. Rates average about $54 per night and there is usually no charge for children under 12. The motel chain has a program called Gold Crown Club International, which carries special services and awards for frequent guests. 1-800-528-1234

- Budgetel offers hotel-like services at motel rates, such as complimentary breakfast delivered to your room, free local phone calls, free incoming fax service, extra-long beds, and remote control TV. Some of the 100 Budgetels have guest laundry and a nearby restaurant. Non-smoking rooms and "leisure suites" with an additional working area are great features. Rates average about $40. 1-800-428-3438

- Comfort Inns offer free lodging to children under age 18 staying in their parents' room, a complimentary continental breakfast, and nonsmoking rooms. Many have swimming pools, fitness facilities, and restaurants or coffee shops on the premises. Rates average about $49. 1-800-228-5150

- Days Inns offers rooms as low as $29 if reservations are made at least 29 days in advance, but generally average around $52. Children under 12 stay for free in their parents' room. Children also eat free when accompanied by an adult who is a registered guest. About 15% of the motels offer suites or below-budget rooms. Some offer free in-room movies, coin laundries, and on-the-premises cocktail lounges. These motels have the best senior citizen discounts in the market, 20% to 40% off the regular rates. 1-800-325-2525

- Econo Lodge has about 766 motels. Many have swimming pools and rates average $36 per night. Rollaway beds cost $5 extra and children under 18 stay free with parents. 1-800-553-2666

- Fairfield Inns are Mariott's addition to the budget market. There are about 125 motels in 34 states. Most have spas with swimming pools and offer complimentary breakfast. Rates range from $29 to $50 and are generally lower on weekends than weeknights. Fairfield Inns are my runaway choice for the best budget hotel because they have the touch of Marriott. Unfortunately, there are not many of them, yet. 1-800-228-2800

- Hampton Inns was the first company to advertise an unconditional satisfaction guarantee. If you are not satisfied with the accommodations or service, you don't pay. This chain offers complimentary continental breakfast in the lobby, free local phone calls, and in-room movie channels. Most have swimming pools and exercise rooms, and those near airports offer free shuttle service. Rates average $49. Third and fourth adults can stay in a room for free. 1-800-426-7866

- HoJo Inns, a spin-off of Howard Johnson's, has about 165 locations around the country. Rates average $40 per night and accommodations vary from property to property. Most have swimming pools. 1-800-446-4656

- La Quinta Inns comprise 215 southwestern-style properties in 29 states. Guests receive free continental breakfast in the lobby, same-day laundry and dry-cleaning for a fee, outdoor swimming pool, fax machine, and free local phone calls. Most offer free shuttle service to nearby airports and have adjacent family restaurants. Rates average $50 a night. If you stay 11 nights at any time, you get one night free. 1-800-531-5900

- Motel 6 is probably the most popular of the motel chains and has about 650 properties. Who can forget the slogan "We'll leave the light on for you?" They offer bare-bones lodging. There is no breakfast, coffee shop, or pictures on the wall. These motels feature an average per-night rate of only $31. Most do have pools and free local phone calls. 1-800-466-8356

- Super 8 Motels are the giant of the motel chain industry with over 1,000 properties in 49 states. Many offer waterbeds and meeting rooms. Others have free continental breakfast, kitchenettes, and swimming pools. They vary in quality and amenities from property to property. Children under 12 stay free. 1-800-800-8000

When you are traveling across the country, first think of staying in a budget motel instead of a more expensive place. Make a few phone calls and do a little footwork, and you'll be able to stay in a comfortable room for a lot less.

Save Money on Your Next Flight

Flying can be a hassle, but it doesn't have to be if you know the inside tips that can make air travel much easier. Here are some great ways to take the turbulence out of the air and save a lot of money too:

- If you travel frequently, you may get bumped off of a plane or get told to go to another gate to book another flight. Instead of making the mad dash to the gate, then having to wait in long lines to get your seat, just pick up the phone and call your travel agent. Ask him or her to book you on the next available flight, or the flight the airline wants you to reschedule on. You will save time and effort and probably get booked faster on your flight than those other poor travelers who don't have your know-how.

- Fly off-peak to get the best fares. Fares on domestic flights are usually the cheapest on Tuesdays, Wednesdays, and Thursdays. Avoid flying between 6 a.m. and 9 a.m. on weekdays, when fares are high because of business traveler demand. For international travel, avoid flying on the weekends when flights are in demand and fares are highest.

- Make the airline reservationist your friend. If you're making your reservation through the airline rather than a travel agent, the reservationist can be your biggest ally. Remember, their job is to get the plane filled, not get you the best deal. Try to call at night and on the weekend when they aren't as busy and have more time to deal with you. Be overly nice and you may just get the best price, or even get them to bend the rules a bit. Most of the time they deal with angry business travelers and someone who is cordial is a refreshing change. Some questions you should ask: Would it be cheaper if I flew at a different time of the day or a different day of the week? Do you know of any special fares that would save me money? Do you offer a family discount on this flight?

- Use a close but less popular airport. For example, if you are visiting Washington, DC, you can save by flying into Dulles rather than into Washington National. Ask your airline or travel agent if there is an alternative airport that might offer better rates. Most of the time these airports are much more pleasant since they are less crowded.

- Buy your tickets from an accredited consolidator only for international flights. You can save up to 40% by using a consolidator (this strategy doesn't work well for domestic flights). Consolidators buy seats at deep discounts and than pass the savings on to you. Your travel agent can be a good source for reputable consolidators. If not, try the Yellow Pages. One common disadvantage to consolidators is that flights may have layovers and tickets are generally nonrefundable. As mentioned earlier, you need to be very careful about which consolidator you use for your foreign flight. This industry has its share of scam artists, so always purchase with a credit card. Never pay with cash or a check.

- Avoid paying extra when you don't have a Saturday night stay. Under the airlines' ridiculous rules, buying two sets of tickets with a Saturday-night stay might actually be cheaper than buying just one set without a Saturday-night stay. Say you live in Chicago and want to visit Orlando for vacation. To use this strategy, simply buy one round-trip ticket that flies you on the day you leave from your home city (Chicago) to your destination (Orlando) and back. Then buy a second round-trip ticket that starts with your destination (Orlando) on the day you want to return, flies to your home (Chicago) and back. When flying, you just use the first ticket from each set. This strategy works when the cheapest Saturday night stay tickets cost less than half the round trip with no Saturday night stay. If it costs you $1,000 for a "non" Saturday night stay, and $400 for each of the Saturday night stay tickets, then you will save $200, plus you'll have two more tickets for another trip! Usually you just have to pay a $50 reservation fee to reuse these other tickets. Confusing enough? The airlines have done it to themselves.

- Join frequent flyer programs and take full advantage of them. You don't necessarily have to be a jet-setter business traveler to benefit from these programs. Often you can get free upgrades and bonuses for just 5,000 miles of travel.

When making your travel arrangements, always ask for discounts or specials available through the airline's partners. These are companies that have set up special promotions on car rentals, hotels, florists, credit cards, etc. Not only do you get great deals in conjunction with air travel with these partners, but you also get frequent flyer miles by using their services.

ACTION LIST:

1. If your travel agent doesn't seem to make an extra effort to try to find you the best deal on airfares and vacation packages, find a new agent. Better yet, spend more time doing your own travel planning and give yourself a chance to learn how to find the best deals.

    Date completed: _____

2. If you are planning a short trip to a city nearby, consider booking on a train for something new and different in travel.

    Date completed: _____

3. For a great travel deal, how about taking a cruise in the Caribbean? You can't beat the relaxation and the quality of service.

    Date completed: _____

4. Next time you are driving across the country, make an extra effort to stay at a budget motel as opposed to a fancier hotel. If you plan ahead, you can make reservations along the entire route and not lose a night's sleep.

    Date completed: _____

CHAPTER 12

Saving in Sickness and Health

> The most valuable of all capital is that invested in human beings.
>
> —Alfred Marshall

The rising cost of health care is enough to make you get sick and put you in the hospital. With the medical industry being a $500 billion annual business, the politicians, insurance companies, and lawyers are all lining up for a piece of the action.

The cost of staying healthy is skyrocketing, and frankly there is no end in sight. If we stay on the present course, we will probably see health care costs rise at about 10% per year for the next ten years. It won't be long before we spend $1 trillion on health care alone. This will represent about 15% of the country's gross domestic product! The key problem in cutting health care costs is the lack of bargains. Let's face it, open-heart surgery is just plain expensive—it is going to cost about the same whether you have it done on the West Coast or the East Coast.

If you have the proper knowledge of health care, however, you can save hundreds of dollars per year and still get good quality care. Here are a few healthy strategies to get you started.

The Cheapest Insurance on Earth

At age 60, some people can look like they're 45 while others at age 45 can look 60. Most of this comes from the fact that we're all prone to certain biological traits. Still, much of the aging process can be controlled by how you take care of yourself and also how you view your age. If you lead a healthy life and stay active, then you can probably prolong your life and possibly keep yourself out of expensive hospitals longer.

We all know what we should do. Eat right, exercise regularly, and keep stress down by getting plenty of relaxation. Living a healthier lifestyle will ultimately save you a lot of money and a lot of emotional worries. Consider the high cost of health care. If you can keep the doctor away as much as possible, you will save bundles of money. Staying in good shape can also make you feel better emotionally, which leads to less stress and less time in the hospital. By taking care of yourself when you're younger, your quality of life will increase tremendously in the older years.

The best way to make sure that your family will be well taken care of in the future is for you to be there! Life insurance is important, but for your quality of life and that of your family, keep yourself in top shape.

Body Wise

To keep your body in great shape, make sure you have a physical once a year. Although a complete physical is expensive, having it will save you money in the long run. Many of today's diseases and illnesses can be alleviated if they're detected early enough. A good doctor will tell you what you need to do to keep your body running efficiently. One of the surest ways to cut medical costs is through preventative care. Get to know your body well enough so you can detect something that's out of whack.

It doesn't cost a lot to eat healthy if you shop correctly. When you eat healthier, you'll increase your physical vitality and improve the quality of your life. It's smarter—from a health and economic view—to buy fresh fruit, vegetables, and breads rather than prepackaged low-fat meals.

Also, make sure you count fat grams in foods rather than calories. Focus on eating whole, fresh foods, with as much fiber and protein and as little fat, salt, and other additives as possible.

Healthy Checkup

In the spring, most communities have health fairs sponsored by hospitals or community health organizations. At these fairs, you can get your cholesterol checked, a blood pressure screening, be tested for colon cancer, etc. These services are done at no charge. Often, preventative tests like these at the doctor's office are not covered by health insurance, so you'll save yourself both a trip to the doctor and the expense. Also, these fairs can be a great way to teach children about science and medicine. Call your local hospital or community health center if you want further information.

Live Long and Prosper

Are you looking to increase your longevity? Here are a few simple life-extending habits:

- Sleep seven to eight hours nightly.

- Keep your weight to no more than 10 pounds over what is recommended for your height, build, and age.

- Get a half hour of moderate aerobic exercise every day by walking, swimming, or participating in some other active sport.

- Don't smoke.

- Eat only three meals a day and plan them out a week in advance.

- Eat as much fat-free food as possible.

- Don't drink, or limit yourself to an ounce of alcohol per day.

One Potato Two

As Mom said, I should eat more potatoes. A potato is virtually fat-free, low in sodium, and a great source of carbohydrates. They're cheap, too. They can usually be bought in five-pound bags for less than the cost of most vegetables. Potatoes, especially the skins, are full of vitamins, minerals, and fiber. But watch out for the toppings, such as sour cream, gobs of butter, and salt. Instead, try putting some fat-free cheese or sour cream on them or some herb seasoning. Also, don't ever fry them. If you visit the library you can find recipes for creative dishes you can make with potatoes.

Pop It

Popcorn is fairly nutritious, low in calories, and reasonably high in fiber. It is also about the cheapest snack that you can buy anywhere. Without added oil or butter, a three-cup serving can cost as little as three cents. I recommend you buy your own kernels and pop it yourself. You may want to use an air popper to get the healthiest popcorn possible and avoid all those fatty oils. If you buy it yourself, you can often find inexpensive bags of generic popcorn. The store-bought microwave brands are expensive unless you can find a special deal. My experience is that there is not much difference between the generic stuff and the so-called gourmet popcorns. Give me a break! This is another example of American marketing ingenuity at its best. Try cheap, healthy popcorn in place of the more expensive potato chips and other snacks.

Smoking Drain

If you are a smoker, now is a great time to stop. You already know about the health risks to yourself and possibly to those around you. Economically, quitting smoking can save you hundreds of dollars per year. If you buy a pack of cigarettes for $2.50 and smoke about a half a pack per day, that's about $300 per year. And the cost is undoubtedly going to go up. It seems that cigarettes are always the first thing that Congress goes after when it's looking for new revenue through sales taxes. It's an expensive habit—both on your lungs and pocketbook—and will only get more expensive as the years roll on.

Curb Your Drug Costs

Over the past decade, most prescription drugs have doubled in cost. In fact, their cost has outpaced inflation by more than six times since 1980. Under one of the many proposed health care reform bills, prescription drug costs will be capped at levels determined by drug manufacturers. This probably won't happen anytime soon, though.

You can fight these mounting costs in several ways:

- Ask for generics whenever you fill a prescription. They are generally 50% lower in price than brand-name drugs. Ask your doctor if buying a generic drug is acceptable when he or she gives you a prescription. Some dosage requirements are very precise, and you may not be able to use a generic drug.

- Check out different pharmacies. Chain stores are generally cheaper in price than corner drug stores and they also have a wider variety of drugs. Comparison shopping can save you as much as 20%.

- Investigate mail-order houses if you use certain drugs frequently. If you have a chronic condition, you can save as much as 15% using these houses.

- Make sure you are taking full advantage of the benefits of your health insurance policy. Many policies have prescription drug benefits, but don't advertise them very well. In fact, it's estimated that over $50 million worth of drugs bought in this country by individuals could have been paid for by insurance.

- Many companies offer prescription drug benefits separate from health insurance policies since prices of drugs have gone up so drastically. Some let you buy at participating drug stores in the area and others are set up with mail-order houses. Check with your employee benefits department and see if they offer a good program. If your company doesn't offer this plan, suggest it.

Prescription Addiction

Doctors are addicted to giving brand-name prescription drugs to their patients. They do this because they are always getting hit up by salespeople pushing one drug or another. They get certain "perks" from pharmaceutical companies if they sell enough of these drugs. Vacations to conferences and great birthday and Christmas gifts are just a few of these. Tell you doctor when he or she is writing your prescription to order a generic if one is available. Any ethical doctor will do this. When he or she fills out the prescription with the brand name, the doctor will then simply check a box to let the pharmacist know that a generic can be used. Generally, generics are about half the cost of name-brand drugs.

Save 50% on Your Health Insurance

The story is starting to get old. The cost of health care keeps going up and up and there doesn't seem to be an end in sight. For many families, good medical coverage is fast becoming one of the greatest expenses next to housing and taxes. The average cost of health insurance for a family of four is a staggering $300 per month. If you are one of the 50% of Americans who do not have an employee-paid plan, then read on.

If you believe that you are always getting great advice from your employer about your health plan, think again. The experts in your company are usually trained by the insurance companies! It is common practice for a large company to arrange a contract with an insurance company that includes full training. That's why you have to get knowledgeable enough to get the maximum protection and pay the least in premiums.

When your agent sold you your last health insurance policy, he or she probably touted the benefits of a low deductible because it reduces your out-of-pocket expenses. It does, on the back end, but what about now? You might be paying as much as $1,500 more per year to have the advantage of paying $750 to $1,000 less if disaster strikes. If you raise your deductible to $1,000, you can save as much as 40% on current low deductible rates. If you put the amount of money you save in an account for just half a year, you will be in a position to make up the extra risk involved with a higher deductible. Remember that the biggest risk associated with your health is the many thousands of dollars it could cost you if an accident occurs, not the small amount of money associated with your deductible.

Next, pick a stop-loss amount (percentage you are responsible for after deductible is met) that is reasonable. I suggest an 80/20 plan up to $5,000. This means that you would be responsible for 20% of costs (after your deductible was met) up to $5,000. Using my suggestions of a $1,000 deductible and an 80/20 stop-loss, your maximum out-of-pocket expenses would be $2,000.

Make sure the insurance company you are dealing with is rated A or better by A.M. Best Company, an independent rating service. You want to feel confident that the company is dependable and pays their claims on time. A good rule of thumb to use is to find a company that operates in at least 40 states nationwide. This means the company is stable and has been around for a while. Never buy insurance from a company licensed only in a few states. Also, talk to several randomly selected policyholders. This is a bit unconventional, but you will learn a lot about the quality of the company's policies by talking to other policyholders.

As with most insurance products, there's a long list of "don't buys" with health insurance. Never buy maternity benefits because they are way overpriced and provide very little coverage. Likewise, dental and prescription drug benefits are better bought separately from your policy since they are also overpriced. Accident coverage can be a good buy if you are very active and prone to an injury like a broken ankle or a torn ligament; otherwise, forget it.

If you are under 65 and you and your family are in good health, I suggest you take a catastrophic outlook on your health care. This means that you should take care of the minor expenses yourself but be completely covered if something major occurs so you won't get wiped out financially. You have the advantage of low premiums and good coverage if something major happens in your family. Buy a policy with the parameters outlined above and use the money you will save to pay for the little expenses like yearly checkups and routine doctor visits. Most likely, you'll still have money left over at the end of the year.

Medigap Protection

Medigap insurance is insurance that picks up what Medicare can't cover. First, you have to decide which benefits you are most likely to need. Many policies cover a variety of services such as nursing home co-payments, out of country emergencies, prescription drugs, etc. You need to understand the premium structure for policies offering similar benefits. Also, check out the cap on premium adjustments. Many companies get you locked into a rate, and then bump the payments 20% or more the second year. Ask for a guarantee of the lowest percentage increase possible. Check to see that the insurer will bill Medicare directly for services not covered so that you won't have to get involved in filing and paying bills yourself.

Group policies for associations and non-profit organizations are your best bet because their rates are generally lower and the benefits are better. To get information on the best insurers, contact a senior counseling association in your region.

Cheap Shades

Cheap sunglasses are really not too cheap. Recent studies have suggested that the expensive name-brand sunglasses don't protect your eyes any more than el cheapos. Optometrists recommend that lenses have proper UV sun protection. Most cheap plastic lenses have UV protection. Just check on the label for the UV seal. Perfectly good and safe sunglasses should cost around $15.

Glass Is Class

If you wear glasses, consider buying good, old-fashioned glass lenses. Plastic lenses provide scratch resistance and are lightweight, but overall, they do not hold up as long as glass. After a few years, plastic lens coatings may start to wear off, and the lenses may get gouged or scratched easily. Glass is hard to scratch and very durable. Also, when your frames give out, you can always take out your glass lenses and just buy a new frame. You can even pick out different frames if they are the same size or smaller than the original ones. Glass can be cut down to fit into any size frame. Get wire metal frames, not plastic. Plastic frames are much more brittle and less forgiving if your glasses get damaged.

Contact Dilemma

If you are a contact lens wearer, visit your eye doctor and request your prescription. Often, your doctor won't give it to you because he or she makes a large profit by selling you lenses. If your doctor refuses, go to another who will give you your prescription. Don't be intimidated by your doctor and prodded into a purchase at the office. Instead, order lenses with your prescription in hand at a local discount store, price club, or through the mail. You save cash and your doctor still gets paid for exam services. Remember, regular visits to your doctor are still important; just buy lenses elsewhere!

Itchy Remedy

For relief of the pain and itching caused by insect bites, poison ivy, sunburn, and other skin irritants, use 100% aloe vera. If you have the plant available, just cut a leaf in half and squeeze out the balm to provide instant relief. You can grow an aloe vera plant inside very easily. If the plant is not available, many discount drug stores sell aloe vera lotions. Look for the ones that have the highest content of the balm. Linseed oil is also another surprising all-purpose skin soother that reduces inflamed tissues and itching.

Coughing Woes

You know it's cold and flu season when just about everyone you talk to either has a bug or has just gotten over something. Here's some advice on buying over-the-counter remedies: Get single-ingredient products such as suppressant, expectorant, or decongestant, depending on the symptoms you have. Generics are as effective as name brands and can save you as much as 40%. Make sure you look at warning labels to see if the remedy causes drowsiness—you can't afford to fall asleep at work. You might try using home remedies such as drinking plenty of fluids, gargling with salt water, or rubbing your chest with pure peppermint oil. If your symptoms persist for more than a week, definitely see a doctor. He or she can prescribe generic antibiotics that should help you.

ACTION LIST:

1. If you haven't already, start yourself on a regular exercise program and begin eating right. Preventative steps are the easiest way to save money and be healthier in the long run.

    Date completed: _____

2. Smoking is a huge drain on your pocketbook and, more importantly, your lungs and entire body. Do whatever you can to stop smoking.

    Date completed: _____

3. Next time you need to buy prescription drugs, opt for generics instead of name-brand drugs. Ask your doctor to specify on your prescription that generics are acceptable.

    Date completed: _____

4. Review your health insurance policy to make sure you are not paying too much. If you have a low deductible, raise your deductible to at least $1,000 to save a significant amount on your premiums.

    Date completed: _____

CHAPTER 13

Living with Lower Housing Costs

> *True value lies in what comes from the ground and also what is built on top of it.*
>
> —Anonymous

Regardless of your vision of your dream home, it can be very unsettling when you start figuring out how you're going to afford the horrific mortgage payments. Looking at the contracts with all those zeros can be a harrowing experience. Plus, all the extra fees for title insurance, escrow, points, and inspections can sometimes add up to thousands or more. Consider what kind of lifestyle you want. Are you looking for a city, suburban, or country life? You may have considerations about the surrounding schools and whether your neighbors have similar interests. How far is the house from your work? Is the environment comfortable?

If you are selling a home, you have to consider the amount of time it will take, the negotiations, and the agent's commission. For these reasons, real estate transactions are one of the most confusing aspects of our lives. But it doesn't have to be that way.

How to Get the Best Mortgage

If you are in the market for a home or have found your dream home, the next step is to make sure you get the right loan. Getting the wrong type of mortgage or overpaying the fees could end up costing you thousands of dollars. Here are some things to watch out for when you talk to your mortgage banker.

With interest rates rising, more and more lenders are getting desperate to make loans. As a result, many people are pushed into unsuitable loans that they don't need. For some time, lenders have been playing around with adjustable-rate mortgages. The mortgage lender comes along and gives you 10 different options, makes it sound confusing, and then hits you with recommendations. Often, this advice is not in your best interest. Never fall for a ridiculously low rate without looking at what it will cost you down the road.

If a mortgage lender can get you to say yes to another half percent, they will pocket more money. Most of the time, giving you the best rate is not in the lender's best interest. The lender generally wants to find out what you can afford before you're quoted an interest rate. Call around to several different lenders in your area and ask for current rates. When you choose one, hold them to this rate. On the day you sign the contracts, get your lender to show you the daily rate card so you know the current percentage rate is the one you committed to.

Also, don't be misled about the APR (annual percentage rate). Many lenders follow different guidelines on how to calculate the APR. Always ask for a detailed, itemized list of estimated closing costs when you hand in your loan application. It's required by law. On closing day, look carefully at the figure called "amount financed" on your settlement papers. If it doesn't equal the principal you are borrowing, minus any points or interest paid up front, ask the lender why. Some fees may have been added in, which means you'll pay more interest.

Be careful of rate lock-ins. Lenders have been known to stretch out the application period if it means they'll get a higher rate than they may have gotten if they locked you in immediately. Only accept this option when you are confident rates are going up and you know your transaction will be processed within the lock-in period.

Also, ask plenty of questions about your closing fees. If any fee looks high or unusual, point it out. It's not uncommon for lenders to make mistakes and overcharge their customers.

Don't accept the lender's word that you are pre-qualified if they just do a "quickie" qualification. If anything comes up between this pre-qualification time and your closing, the mortgage company can reject your application. If a flaw in your credit history turns up or information was incorrect on pre-qualification, you may be out of luck. Make sure you go to a lender that does extensive pre-qualifying so that there are no surprises later.

If you can put at least 20% down on your home, do it. If you don't, most lenders will require that you purchase mortgage insurance, which is expensive and is often non-cancelable. If you have no choice, make sure that there is a clause in your mortgage that allows you to cancel the premiums after you have built up sufficient equity in your home.

Lots of homeowners pay down their mortgage principal every month to save thosands in interest charges over the long haul. The problem is that many lenders can't figure out how to credit this money to your principal. It sounds crazy but bank computer systems aren't generally designed to deal with prepayment of principal. If you want to prepay, ask your lender if it is acceptable and what procedure to follow to do it. Generally you need to send a separate check marked "principal only" for the bank to credit the amount correctly; otherwise, the extra money is put into an escrow account and you won't save yourself a dime.

Don't always take the advice of your real estate agent about which is the best lender to use. Often, agents have a relationship with selected lenders and they receive special treatment or in some cases, even money (this is illegal). Do plenty of searching yourself so that you feel completely comfortable with your lender.

Finally, make sure the lender you go through has an excellent reputation and is in sound financial shape. There are lenders going out of business every day and it is up to you to check the stability of the firm. To find this information, simply ask them for recent financial statements that they give to shareholders. This information will tell you all you need to know about the company's liquidity. Remember, you are much more likely to have a good experience with a lender that has been recommended or has done thousands of loans than if you go to an inexperienced lender.

Down and Dirty

I'm often asked by future homeowners what is the ideal amount to put down on a home that they are purchasing. It is hard to give a specific figure because there are so many variables involved.

If you want to trade up to the highest-priced house you can buy, or if it's your first home, then you should put as little down as possible. In other words, take the most you can from the bank, assuming you have the cash flow to support it. In the 80s, it was not uncommon to see a lot of "nothing down" deals. In the current environment, 15% to 20% down is average.

If you have enough cash in savings to put more down on your mortgage, the amount of the down payment should be determined by the investment return you can get elsewhere. Compare the interest cost on your mortgage to the expected return on another investment. If the investment is taxable, take this into account: For example, if your mortgage is at 9%, then you should be getting two or three percentage points more on your investment to make a smaller mortgage worth it. Try to look at these investments considering an after-tax basis. You may find, for example, that the after-tax return on a tax-free municipal bond exceeds the after-tax cost of the mortgage. Don't forget to look at all fees associated with your loan and also your investment fees such as brokerage costs.

You should also consider that putting money in your home ties that money up, so you're losing liquidity and flexibility with those funds. You could be squeezed financially if an emergency crops up or you come across an outstanding investment opportunity. Many people feel like their net worth drops when they don't have investable funds or cash. If all your money is tied up in a home, it's hard to gauge exactly how much you really have.

In general, it's best to focus on the big picture. If you were to purchase a home and deplete all your investment savings, then you could put yourself in a very tight spot. Putting 20% down on a home is a good starting point, but this money shouldn't make you house-poor. If you feel you can handle more than the required amount down, look at different scenarios starting with 5% increments. For instance, see how it would impact your financial picture if you put 25% down, or 30%, etc.

Finally, there are some people who can afford the luxury of buying a home all in cash. This can be a good idea if it doesn't deplete your entire savings, and you have a significant, monthly cash flow that is reliable. The cash flow can help to replenish lost savings.

Estimating Mortgage Payments

The following table is an easy way to help you calculate what your monthly mortgage payments will be for every $1000 you borrow, not including insurance or taxes. For example, if you were to borrow $100,000 at 7.5% on a 30-year note, your monthly payment would be approximately $700.00 (100 × $7). You can quickly figure the cost difference between a 15-year note and 30-year note using this chart:

Monthly Payment Per $1,000

Interest Rate	15-Year	30-Year
5%	$7.91	$5.37
5.25%	$8.04	$5.52
5.5%	$8.17	$5.68
5.75%	$8.30	$5.84
6%	$8.44	$6.00
6.25%	$8.57	$6.16
6.5%	$8.71	$6.32
6.75%	$8.85	$6.49
7%	$8.99	$6.66
7.25%	$9.13	$6.83
7.5%	$9.28	$7.00
7.75%	$9.42	$7.17
8%	$9.56	$7.34
8.25%	$9.71	$7.52
8.5%	$9.85	$7.69
8.75%	$10.00	$7.87
9%	$10.15	$8.05
9.25%	$10.30	$8.23
9.5%	$10.45	$8.41
9.75%	$10.60	$8.60
10%	$10.75	$8.78

House Appeal

Don't buy a home if:

- There is extensive water damage, especially to structural beams.
- The house is not hooked up to the city sewer system or needs a new cesspool.
- It needs a new roof and the seller won't pay for it.
- The building is structurally unsound due to poor workmanship or poor materials.
- There is evidence of termite infestation or the house is built on a cliff.

All these things could require extensive and expensive repairs. Nothing is worse than falling in love with a house that is unsound and then thinking you can "fix it up." Go on to the next house that doesn't have these same problems.

Fannie Mae Flash

The Federal Home Loan Mortgage Corporation (Fannie Mae) is currently testing a new system that will allow for instant mortgage approval. The advantage to this system is that the application process will be streamlined and save the consumer money. The applicant's information will be entered in a centralized computer that will electronically check all credit agencies and their credit risk, assess appraisal data on the property, and have a yes or no within four minutes! Funds could be made available in two days. This system is expected to help cut costs in other areas of the loan process as well, and should be on-line across the country sometime in 1997.

Slicing Your Mortgage

If the idea of paying thousands of dollars in interest on your mortgage makes you ill, look for ways to cut those finance charges down to size.

The best and easiest way to accomplish this is to switch your mortgage over to a bi-monthly plan. This works by making half your normal monthly payments every two weeks. By doing this, you pay one extra payment a year, which will cut as much as 10 years off your mortgage. On a $100,000 mortgage you will save about $75,000 in interest.

However, not all mortgage companies will do this. If you follow some simple strategies, you'll have a good shot at convincing them to let you go on a bi-monthly plan. Write an impressive letter stating that you would like to amend your mortgage agreement (enclose a copy) to include bi-monthly payments as an option. Explain that you would like those payments credited to your account immediately upon their receipt and that any overpayments will be credited to principal only. Tell them you will consider the payment plan to be agreed to if they do not notify you within one month.

If your bank or mortgage company refuses to comply, don't give up. If enough pressure is applied, they may just accept your proposal to get rid of the problem. A short letter from a lawyer friend might just be the ticket to put the lender over the edge.

If the lender is being stubborn and all this fails, you can still make extra principal payments to help reduce your mortgage. Have your banker or mortgage company run you an amortization schedule that tells you how much of each payment is principal and how much is interest. Every month, make your regular payment and also write a separate check for the next month's principal amount. Write on the check that it is for principal only. This can cut finance charges by thousands over the years.

Another simpler method is to figure out what you can afford to pay in extra principal every month and religiously send that in to help pay down the mortgage. I send in an extra $100 per month and have figured out that my mortgage will be paid off 13 years earlier. I'll save a whopping $47,000 in interest.

Still another way is to divide your monthly payment by 12 and every month send this amount to pay down your principal. For instance, if your mortgage payment is $800 per month, you would divide this figure by 12. You would send an extra $66 each month to pay down your mortgage principal.

Still, bi-weekly mortgages are more advantageous because once you begin paying, you don't really notice any extra money going out. But you must be disciplined and make two payments a month. It's worth the time and energy because you'll own your home that much sooner. Remember that if you do go on a bi-monthly plan, it will be much less of a bite to make two payments a month rather than one whole payment on the 1st of the month.

Building a New Home

If you are planning to build a house, shop around for the best builder. Estimates for the same house can differ by as much as 15%. On a $150,000 home, that's a difference of of $20,000. Price is a big factor, but not the only one. Check the builder's quality of work by visiting homes constructed by them. Talk to several customers. Ask the builder for an approximate cost per square foot. If you are evaluating several different builders, this is a good way to gauge if the added cost per foot is worth what you will gain in quality.

I recommend staying with one of the builder's designs because several of these houses have probably been built already, so costs are lower. A custom-built house always costs more than you expected and may not turn out quite how you envisioned.

Tap Your Home Equity

When you borrow money, always look for the lowest interest rate. Using your home's equity is usually a great way to get a low-interest loan, if your mortgage rate is about 8.25% to 9.75%. The interest up to $100,000 is currently tax deductible, no matter how you spend the loan money. When you get a home equity loan, you have to keep in mind that you are putting your house up for collateral, so you'd better be certain you can pay the loan back.

You can get two types of loans if you are thinking of using your equity: through a home equity loan, or a home equity line of credit. If you choose a home equity loan, it's just like a mortgage. You will get a lump sum of money and then have to make regular monthly payments. If you choose a line of credit, you take only the money you need and make payments based on the amount you borrow.

It may be a better idea to get a home equity loan rather than a line of credit. The interest rate on the equity loan is much cheaper, and so are the fees. Home equity lines usually are more expensive because it costs the bank more to do the administrative work. The bank often charges annual account fees and will also charge you up-front points for the entire amount of the line, even though you may draw only a small amount to begin with. Also, an open line is often tempting to use as a checkbook—one with a big balance! Many lines have variable interest rates that can fluctuate wildly, making them even more unattractive.

You should get a home equity loan only for a good reason. Some examples are consolidating debt, paying college costs, home improvements, buying a car with cash, or paying medical expenses. Resist the temptation to use your loan to pay for a vacation or buy a pleasure boat. By the way, don't purchase a loan that restricts what you can pay for with your money. These kinds of loans are very inflexible.

Always get a fixed-rate home equity loan. With a fixed rate, you are protected against fluctuations in the market. A variable-rate loan can become a hardship if your interest rate shoots up 2%. Since home equity loans generally run 2% over prime to begin with, these fluctuations could be devastating to your budget.

Many banks offer different home equity loan programs. Ask friends and relatives if they have gotten loans recently and do a little shopping around. Beware of the small print in many loan agreements. Although most home equity loans are very similar to mortgages, many banks have used their marketing skills to hide fees in the tiny type. Avoid a higher rate that kicks in after a period of time.

Here are some questions to ask so that you don't get burned:

- Is there a balloon payment due? (I wouldn't even consider it if there is.)
- Can the lender change the terms of the loan at any point in the payment period? The lender should provide you with a complete disclosure statement about the home equity loan.

A low interest rate is not the sole reason to get a loan. It's important to take into account the service you will receive from a bank or loan company and how the loan is structured. The industry has many companies with questionable practices. The peace of mind that you get with a well-established firm can make the difference whether you will sleep well at night.

Moving Made Easy

Terrible movers are commonplace in today's world of the fast buck. Here are some common problems with movers and how to avoid them:

Problem: You get socked with an add-on bill at the end of the move because it took the movers longer than expected to get aunt Mae's antique bed up to the third floor.

Solution: Make sure that all costs are written down in the estimate you receive and ask whether there are any hidden costs. Have the mover write on the estimate, "There are no extra costs associated with this proposal," and then both parties should initial it. Tell the mover about any places in your new home that you think may be difficult for them to handle. Above all, use a mover that has an excellent reputation in your town, preferably one that has been referred to you by a friend or relative. If you have to pay a few extra bucks, do it.

Problem: You have a prized oak table that you don't want damaged.

Solution: To avoid any handling problems, watch the loading and unloading. All movers will be much more careful if they know you're watching. Be courteous about it and don't get in their way. Examine all your belongings and furniture before you sign the final check so you don't have to extract money from the company when you find a problem later.

Problem: The movers don't show up, or are late.

Solution: Call the company if they are any more than 30 minutes late. If they don't show up and it costs you money because of the delay, demand to be compensated. If you have major problems receiving any refunds from them, contact your local consumer protection agency.

The Artist's Touch

To add a new look to your home, consider changing some of the artwork. Paintings can be expensive, so try buying low-priced prints, maps, quilts, antique plates, or platters. I have seen framed drawings by children that are quite interesting. Frame these art-works yourself and you can save a bundle. Check the local hobby shop for supplies and how-to books. Definitely avoid paying a frame store to do framing for you.

New House Cleanup

If you are thinking about building a new home, ask the builder if you can do the post-construction cleanup on the job site. Not only will this save you money but you and a few of your family members helping can do a great job. Often, contractors hire inefficient and costly cleaners to do the job. They may not clean up paint splatters, dust in corners, and so forth. Depending on the size of the job, you may save several hundred dollars.

Property Tax Fiasco

Like many Americans, you may be faced with enormous property taxes this year. When you get the bill, you'll react with disgust and pay it like all the other bills, thinking there's nothing you can do since it's a tax. Wrong. Many counties make mistakes when it comes to calculating property tax levies. Often the dimensions of the land are inaccurate, skewing calculations. The descriptions of the land or the buildings on it might also be wrong. Improvements can be calculated incorrectly. There are many things that can go wrong in evaluating properties. Call a reputable attorney and inquire about your rights. Many homeowners have been pleasantly surprised when they pushed the assessor's office up against the wall and found that they were right.

Time-Share Traps

Many owners of time-shares in beach and ski areas are becoming more and more disenchanted with their purchases. They have found that committing themselves to the same resort at the same time every year becomes too restrictive. Also, they often find they have overpaid.

To avoid some of these common problems, make sure you follow these rules when shopping: Locate one of the companies that act as swapping agents with other resorts in different areas, especially where you think you may want to vacation. Ask how often owners from your resort swap with the one you're interested in. Also, insist on talking with at least three current time-share owners at the property you are buying at.

Never pay more than 10 times the going rate for a good hotel room or apartment rental at the same vacation time and in the same area you are looking to purchase. You may also consider getting in on a new property since most builders are eager to "sell out" as soon as possible. The rates are usually very good. Check their references so you will feel comfortable about maintenance and competent management.

Choose a one- or two-bedroom unit. Smaller or larger units are usually harder to sell or exchange. A two-bedroom unit is ideal because it works well for a small family or two adult couples. Pick a time during peak season because it will be more negotiable.

Look for areas that have special zoning because of geography. Vail, Colorado, for example, has a moratorium on further time-share development. You may have to pay more in these areas, but your property will be more marketable if you want to sell or exchange. Beware of resorts that are too hard to reach or in the back woods. Your time-share will be harder to rent, swap, or sell.

ACTION LIST:

1. If you are considering buying a home soon, put as much money as you can toward a down payment. Make sure it doesn't strap your savings plan, though. Having all your savings tied up in home equity is not a good idea.

    Date completed: _____

2. If you want to pay down your mortgage as a part of your savings plan, check into bi-monthly mortgage payments or simply make extra principal payments once a month.

    Date completed: _____

3. Take out a home equity loan if you want to consolidate debts or take advantage of a good investment opportunity. The interest will be tax-deductible and will in effect lower your interest rate.

    Date completed: _____

4. When hiring a mover, check several references. Make sure they are registered with the Better Business Bureau in your area and find out if there is an outlandish number of complaints registered.

    Date completed: _____

PART III

$ensible Money Management

CHAPTER 14

Investing and Banking Basics

> *Some men worship rank, some worship heroes, some worship God, and over all these ideals they dispute ... but they all worship money.*
>
> —*Mark Twain*

Now that you have the *$ensible $aver's* advice down pat, it's time to move on to investing. Until now, you may have been putting a few extra bucks in your savings account at the bank, nervous about doing anything else with those hard-earned dollars.

That reaction is not surprising, given the numerous investment options now available. Choosing the right investments is difficult. As you read this book, countless people are getting burned by slick-talking brokers and financial advisors. My philosophy on investing is this: Keep it simple and do it yourself. You have no reason to spend countless hours of your week trying to sort out and track your investments. You can find ways to make a good return and still be able to sleep at night. And you don't need to pay an investment advisor if you are willing to do a little legwork yourself. By doing some reading and research and concentrating on selecting simple investments, you will do just fine over the long run. You will also have the added benefit of saving money on fees and commissions.

Great Ways to Invest Small Amounts of Cash

People are constantly complaining that they never have enough money to spare to start a savings plan. Even if you have some extra money, you might be uncertain where to invest it. In fact, you don't need large sums of money to start an investment program.

Even if your money is tight and you can afford to invest only $25 per month, you can still accumulate substantial amounts over the years. If you invested $25 every month for 30 years, and the money earned 8% interest, you would accumulate a tidy $45,000 in savings. Not bad for less than one dollar per day. Here are some of the best ways to invest small amounts of money to get the maximum returns over time:

- Take a specified dollar amount and invest it in a no-load mutual fund each month. (No-load funds are explained later in this chapter.) If you plan to keep the money in the fund for six years or longer, put it in a growth stock fund. That way, you take advantage of the natural ups and downs in the stock market. Historically, the stock market has outperformed any other type of investment over the long term.

- Pay off the balances on your credit cards. I can't think of a faster way to get 18% to 21% interest on your money. If your balances are high, use a portion of your savings to pay off the balances.

- Buy a U.S. savings bond. Even though the interest rate is generally low on savings bonds, they are still a good way to get started investing. Series EE bonds enable you to buy a bond for half the face value and then redeem it at maturity for full value. Many companies even allow automatic payroll deductions so you can buy a savings bond without paying commissions.

- Pay extra principal toward your mortgage. By paying a small amount each month toward the principal on your mortgage, you can dramatically reduce the length of your mortgage, by as much as 10 or 15 years. Simply write out a separate check to your mortgage company marked *principal only*. For example, if you have a $100,000, 30-year mortgage at 9% interest, and you pay an extra $50 per month toward principal, you will save about $50,000 in interest and pay the mortgage off seven years earlier. Keep your canceled checks so at the end of the year you can verify how much you put toward your principal. Mortgage companies are notorious for crediting these payments wrong. Also, be careful not to make this practice your only source of saving. You need to have money available for emergencies and long-term financial goals. If your money is all tied up in your home, you're in trouble.

- Go to a discount book store once a month and invest in a book on personal finance. If you read one book a month on money matters, you will be very well educated by the end of the year. Better yet, just go to the library and get books for free. Most libraries have extensive sections and periodicals on personal finance matters. The more educated you are on personal finances, the less likely you are to be fooled by some unscrupulous advisor. Making decisions about where to invest your money will be easier.

- Join a local investment club. These clubs are groups of individuals who get together and invest their pooled funds. Members are usually non-professionals but often have pros at the helm. Surprisingly, many clubs have had incredible results. I guess two (or more) heads are definitely better than one. You can find out about investment clubs in your area by calling the National Association of Investors Corporation at (810) 583-6242. You can also ask your banker or investment advisor if they know of any good clubs.

- Swap money-saving investment ideas with friends and neighbors. If you are adventurous, start your own savings club. Again, the two heads concept is great. Have members jot down ideas for saving and investing, then meet once a month to share them. Ideas don't need to be limited to the small things. This concept is different from investment clubs because you're just sharing ideas, not investing.

- Buy stock directly from a company in which you may already have an investment interest. Most major companies offer a *dividend-reinvestment plan*. With these plans, you can buy new shares of the stock without paying commissions if you already have stock. Some companies even offer discounts off current quoted rates. The Standard and Poor's Annual Directory lists all the companies offering dividend-reinvestment plans. You can access this information at your local library.

Mutual Fund Mania

I am a big supporter of mutual funds for a number of reasons. Mutual funds are one of the simplest investments to get into and manage. With some funds, you can make an initial investment of only $50. Mutual funds have a huge pool of money—including your money—in the fund, and the professional managers invest it wisely. You don't do anything other than pay about a 1% annual fee of the fund's value for this professional management. Most of us don't have the time or inclination to track the market and our investments every month. That's what mutual funds do for us. The fee is taken out of your holdings in the fund so you don't need to write any separate checks.

Before you invest, decide what your investment objectives are. You may want to consult an investment advisor to determine your goals, but you can do it on your own by reading some good publications on investing. Are you looking for growth, income, capital preservation, or a combination of all these? When you have your objectives in mind, you can narrow down your fund choices.

As far as performance of the fund, you want to look at the 3- and 5-year performance records. If you are a long-term investor, try to find the 10- and 15-year performance of the fund as well. You can find these performance records in many different finance magazines. Never invest in a fund that has just skyrocketed for one year and has an average record for previous years. Odds are the fund is a shot in the dark.

I highly recommend no-load mutual funds (no commissions) because on average their performance is every bit as good as commissioned funds, and you may as well have all your money at work. Some load (commission) funds charge as much as 8.5%. Also, stay away from funds that are either too small (below $50 million) or too large (over $2 billion). When funds are too small or large, they cannot adequately diversify.

Some discount brokers are now offering no-load mutual funds through one account that you set up with them. The benefit is that you can have several mutual funds and trade them out of one account for easier bookkeeping. The funds pay the broker's fee for your investment, so you pay nothing.

Keep an eye on the performance of your fund and make sure you are keeping up with fund sector averages. If you continue to lag behind normal performances, you may want to reevaluate your fund investment choice.

These high-quality mutual fund families are my favorites:

Twentieth Century Investors (800) 345-2021

Vanguard (800) 851-4999

Fidelity (800) 544-8888

T. Rowe Price (800) 638-5660

Write or call any of these mutual fund companies for more information, including a prospectus.

Dark Secrets of Mutual Funds

Now that I have touted the benefits of mutual funds, you need to be aware of some pitfalls before you blindly put money into a fund:

- Mutual fund marketing can be very misleading to the average investor. Many funds advertise heavily when the fund has performed well for two or three years. A barrage of ads in financial newspapers and magazines can generate millions and millions of new investment dollars for the fund. However, you should be more concerned with the fund performance over the past 5 to 7 years, not just the last year or two. The reality is that many funds that do well for just a few years may be the dogs in the coming years. Always check out a fund's average performance over 3, 5, 10, and 15 years before you invest.

- Beware of mutual fund performance claims that are stretched out over 20, 25, or 30 years. Look for performance figures that go no further than 15 years. You may see charts that show you what $1,000 or more would be worth if you had invested 20 or more years ago. The reality is that a large percent of gains calculated in dollar terms is due to inflation and the reduced value of today's dollar. Also, a fund may have had a spectacular gain in that period of time and still be riding on figures from two decades ago to help make current gains look good. The best strategy is to look at year-by-year performances for about the last 15 years. Pay special attention to any years that were down significantly and take a gut check. If you can't stomach huge losses that some mutual funds commonly have, then look elsewhere. Also, bear in mind that as I write this book, the economy is still in the biggest bull market in history; many of these funds' outstanding gains are calculated since the early 1980s when the bull market started. Things may change for the worse and fund performances will not be the same as in past years.

- Some mutual funds give the impression that all investment decisions are made by an expert management committee. In fact, one manager usually is making the final decisions. Nothing is inherently wrong with that arrangement, but you need to watch out for changes in the performance of the fund, especially if the fund manager leaves. You may want to switch your money out of the fund at that point if you don't feel comfortable with the new manager.

- Your fund may be gambling millions of dollars that the market may go a certain way. It is not uncommon for some mutual funds to go out on a limb with very risky investments to try to make a name for themselves (or if things backfire, lose their name). Remember that the mutual fund industry has become very competitive in the last several years, and many new funds will do whatever it takes to get a market share. Again, look for past performance and also keep your risk tolerance in mind. If you want stability in a fund, don't look at an aggressive growth fund.

- Beware of funds that have a 7% or greater stake in any single company. (You can find this information in the fund's prospectus or in a recent annual report.) If a fund has a huge stake in any one investment and they need to sell off this investment quickly when the market changes, the fund can lose substantial value. I generally like to see well-diversified funds.

- Keep meticulous records of all your transactions. If you are awestruck by the mess of papers, hire a good accountant to make some sense of your investments. If you use the popular dollar cost averaging strategy—where you invest a certain amount month after month in a mutual fund—you may have trouble figuring your tax liability when you sell your shares.

- Mutual funds make oodles of money. Stay away from funds that try to extract more than a 1% or maximum 2% management fee. Also, watch out for 12b-1 fees. This fee pays for nothing more than marketing the mutual fund. Why should you have to spring for this bill? Higher fees cut into your return. If the fund asks you to vote for a higher fee, write them and ask how you can help the fund cut costs. The reason that over 3,500 mutual funds exist is because they are low-overhead, high-return propositions.

By being aware of some of these pitfalls, you will be on more solid ground when it comes time to invest.

A Few Investments to Avoid

There are lots of investments out there, and it is hard to judge which ones may the best for you. There are some investments that are just not good under any circumstances, and I have listed them here so you don't get taken by an advisor:

- *CMOs or collateralized mortgage obligations*—CMOs are pools of mortgages issued by government agencies like Ginnie Mae, Fannie Mae, and Freddie Mac. These agencies guarantee payment of principal and interest. Many unscrupulous brokers give these investments a AAA rating, meaning they are very safe. No such rating exists for these types of debt obligations.

  The trouble begins when institutions start to carve up the mortgages, dividing the principal payment from the interest, and then putting the mortgages back into some type of accelerated bond pool. The more slices in the bond pool, the worse it is for the average investor like you and me. The real winners here are the institutions that did the slicing to begin with. Their "left-overs" are then sold to us, or you might say thrown to the hogs.

  I haven't even mentioned the threat of fluctuating interest rates. CMOs are pools of home mortgages, and when mortgage interest rates fall, homeowners refinance. If interest rates drop 2%, an 8% CMO that was sold to you and estimated to mature in 1999 may indeed mature in just a few years. Then you will be forced to invest at lower rates. When interest rates rise, mortgage prepays slow down. The broker can only guess at the average mortgage life on your CMO. Brokers make these guesses sound like a guaranteed bond maturity date. With a 2% rise in interest rates, the CMO that was estimated to mature in 1999 wouldn't come due until 22 years later! Also, to make matters worse, rising interest rates dramatically erode the value of the CMO, leaving you high and dry in several years.

- *IPOs or initial public offerings*—An IPO is nothing more than the first shares of stock offered to the public. The newspapers are full of these great IPO successes, but the little guy rarely wins. The simple fact is that if a broker is offering the stock, something is terribly wrong. It's common knowledge on Wall

Street that only the big boys (pension funds, institutions, mutual funds, and large traders on the floor) get the hot IPOs. You don't stand a chance of buying in unless you have some major bucks.

If you are absolutely convinced that a company is a great buy, wait several months after the stock has come onto the market. Then you can buy the stock for its true value and avoid the major fluctuations inherent with all IPOs. This way, you know whether the stock is another Microsoft or just a flash in the pan. You have no reason to rush into any stock; good companies remain good over time.

- *Brokerage WRAP Accounts*—These accounts charge a flat percentage fee of your balance to cover all commissions and fees. They are called WRAP accounts because all your investments are wrapped into one account. I don't like WRAP accounts because you're often charged as much as 5% for these accounts. You can get the same stock-picking expertise in a good mutual fund for less than 1%. Tracking the performance of a mutual fund also is much easier. More and more brokerage firms are starting to mix the institutional investors' performance with performance of private portfolio accounts. This mix helps the firm show off a strong track record, but finding your true rate of return is almost impossible. Stick with much simpler and less expensive mutual funds.

Avoid the Loss

If you are one of those people who likes to invest in individual stocks, remember it is easier for a stock to lose value than to recover from a loss. If a stock drops 10%, it needs to rise 11% just to attain its original value. A stock that drops 50% needs to rise 100% to attain its original value! Not many stocks double in value in a short period of time. You can see that the key to successful investing is to avoid the big loss. When buying a stock, figure out the biggest loss you can afford. Set a stop-loss at about 8% under the value for which you buy the stock. You are smarter to take the loss and move on to greener pastures than to ride the stock lower thinking it will rebound. Keep losses small and let winners ride, and you will come out ahead even if you pick more losers than winners. You can use this strategy for mutual funds also if you invest for the short term.

Bond's the Name

Most people who have investment capital diversify their investment portfolios to protect themselves. If you are in cash or cash equivalents, stocks and bonds, then you won't get nailed if one market segment takes a beating.

The stock market gets a great deal of attention because of the whopping gains some stocks and stock mutual funds have posted in the last several years. One thing about stocks is that they are easy to understand. If the stock goes up, you make money. If it goes down, you lose money. The majority of people invest in stocks for long-term gains. If you are a short-term investor, want income, or just want to protect what you have, bonds are the game. Unfortunately, most people don't know exactly how bonds work. The following paragraphs provide a primer course on bonds.

You can invest in bonds through bond mutual funds, corporate bonds, treasuries, or municipal bonds. Bonds are made available because some corporate or governing agency needs to borrow money to keep afloat. The agency issues bonds and agrees to pay the money back to the person who wants to buy the issue. What's special about a bond investment is that you are guaranteed a fixed amount, or income, when the bond matures.

Federal and state municipal bonds have certain tax advantages, and corporate bonds are totally taxable. Bonds can go up in value, which makes you liable for capital gains. Maturity dates vary in bonds; a *maturity period* is the period of time that elapses before the issuer needs to pay all your principal back. Short-term maturity dates are generally 3 years or less; long-term maturity dates are 10 years or more. Intermediate terms are between 3 and 10 years.

If you purchase a bond for $100 that has a 6% interest rate, that bond can fluctuate in value according to interest rate changes. If the interest rate on your bond rises and you want to sell it, you get less for the bond. It is important to realize that any interest rate fluctuation can have an effect on your bond price.

Much debate occurs on whether to purchase individual bonds or to invest in bond funds. I feel that they are really two different types of investments. Individual bonds are much less speculative than bond funds because you can keep track of your security directly and you know the investment outcome. You can expect to receive an exact amount of income at a specified time.

Bond mutual funds, on the other hand, are a pooling of thousands of different bond issues. The income is not fixed, nor is the amount of money you receive when you decide to redeem the bond fund shares. Bond funds can be very volatile because the fund has so many bonds. They can either appreciate or depreciate in value over a given length of time. However, the advantage to a bond fund is its immediate liquidity. If you need your money right away, you just call the fund and liquidate what you need. You have more liquidity problems buying individual bonds.

Buying individual bonds can be expensive. Most bonds have minimum purchases of $5,000. To diversify in different bonds, you need a lot of money. You usually can buy into bond mutual funds in the $1,000 range.

If you need to have a fixed income and know the value of your bond at all times, buy individual bonds. If you are seeking a more liquid but more volatile type of bond investment (with the prospect of higher returns), consider a bond fund. If you are interested in bond mutual funds, check the most recent issue of a personal finance magazine for the best performers. If you prefer individual bond issues, contact a local broker.

The Inflation Bug

I need to tell you about a very disturbing risk called *purchasing-power risk*. Even if you own the most conservative investments in the world and are confident that your money won't fluctuate, you will lose more than you think because the money you receive when you cash out will buy a lot less. You are a victim of the ever-shrinking dollar.

Inflation is the culprit. Let's say you purchase a $10,000 five-year certificate of deposit and spend the interest income. Inflation is running about 5% per year. When you get your $10,000 back, it buys only $7,800 worth of goods and services. Even if you invested the interest in a safe vehicle, you come out behind.

Investing all your money in debt obligations such as bonds exposes you to this purchasing-power risk. The bottom line is that because your interest rate does not change, the income you receive remains flat while your cost of living increases. Therefore, investing solely in debt instruments may not be as conservative as you thought.

What everyone needs, old and young, is a component in their portfolio that keeps pace with inflation. Most common stocks do, except in the early stages of heightened inflation, because companies are able to raise their prices to maintain returns on product investments. As profits grow, so do dividends and capital gains to investors, so you're staying ahead of inflation. This growth makes common stock a far superior investment over the long haul than debt obligations. Since 1928, U.S. stocks have outpaced inflation 100% of the time, whereas bonds have outpaced inflation only 28% of the time.

In some cases, rental real estate can be an even better investment than common stocks to outpace inflation. You often can pass inflationary costs for operating expenses along to tenants. Many investors buy real estate when they expect inflation to rise, which often creates a self-fulfilling prophecy. If you are willing to take on the added responsibilities and risk associated with owning real estate, you might consider investing some assets into good income-producing property. Overall, for an average investor, real estate returns are about equal to stock market returns over time. If you become a proficient real estate investor, you often can far outpace the return from common stocks.

Gold is often considered an inflation hedge, but its value fluctuates wildly in good and bad times. If you want to own gold, you need to have a strong stomach. Be prepared to keep the gold for at least 20 years to see any kind of true appreciation.

Although the stock market is not the only investment that enables you to keep up with inflation, common stocks can be the easiest and most efficient way to stay ahead of the game.

The Lure of Money Managers

Professional money managers come in all different shapes and sizes. There is the stock broker, the commissioned financial planner, the fee-only financial planner, the mutual fund manager, and more. In a world full of investment management options and thousands of products, making good choices is sometimes difficult.

As I have said before, I recommend that you take the time to educate yourself about personal finances, especially investments. If you spend just a few hours a week reading materials relating to your money, you can make many investment and saving choices yourself and save on commissions and fees.

If you just can't get yourself to swallow this information or you have so much money you don't know what to do with it (a problem we all would like to have), you may choose to go to a manager. Keep in mind these important things:

- Look twice before you leap at a manager who has slick brochures and promises a 20% to 30% return on your money every year. The odds are that the manager is doctoring the figures in his or her favor, not yours.

- Be careful of the financial planner who charges commissions in the 8% range. This is way too much to pay for financial advice. I recommend that you not go to a commissioned planner anyway. Quite often these people give advice tainted by the latest product paying high commissions. A fee-only financial planner is a great route to go if you want honest, unbiased recommendations about where to put your money. Check out several planners in your area and compare investment philosophies and fees.

Seven Great Questions to Ask Your Money Manager

1. Does this investment match my goals, as you understand them?

2. How much risk is involved in this investment and what could go wrong?

3. How much commission do you charge and can I get a discount?

4. Is there a comparable investment that would cost me less?

5. Are any hidden fees involved with this transaction?

6. Taking the commission into consideration, how far does the investment need to go up before I start making money?

7. How liquid is this investment? How fast can you sell it if necessary?

- I am not a big fan of buying individual stocks unless you can diversify heavily and have sage advice. If you want to buy individual stocks, educate yourself about the market and go to a discount broker to make your own trades. Most stock brokers cannot pick stocks any better than you, and they charge hefty fees for their advice.

- I am a big fan of no-load mutual funds because you're giving your money (even if you don't have much) to a professional manager. For the average Joe like you and me, this is the best path to follow.

Beware the Commissioned Salesperson

Quite often I hear horror stories about how people are taken by salespeople who sold them cars, insurance, investments, houses, etc. We all encounter a host of these self-proclaimed "experts" in our lifetime. Most are honest, and are held to certain ethical standards by their industry. Every industry has its share of con artists, though, so keep in mind who these people are working for.

Few car salespeople will tell you about a recent recall due to a car's faulty fuel injector. It would be unwise because it could mean a lost sale and whether their kids will eat this week.

Few stockbrokers will tell you to stay out of the stock market, even if the economic climate clearly warrants it. To do so means no commissions.

An insurance agent is likely to sell you the most expensive insurance policy possible, even when it's not needed. It means more money in his or her pocket.

It's simply human nature. Most salespeople are not greedy, uncaring people, but individuals just like you and me trying to do the best for themselves and their families. They want to keep their jobs by focusing on their financial picture, not yours.

As the saying goes, "let the buyer beware." You are the only person who will put your financial well-being first. How do you protect your interests with so many people trying to grab your wallet?

First, be aggressive in asking questions and demand answers in plain English. Don't worry about being overbearing. It's your right since they are asking for business. Remember, you have no one to blame but yourself if you walk out of a store or office feeling as though you've been taken.

Arm yourself with the facts. A little knowledge can go a long way when dealing with salespeople. Before you make a major purchase, go down to the local library (the $ensible $aver's heaven) and spend an hour researching the product you are buying. This can save you hundreds or thousands of dollars in product costs and commissions.

Check *Consumer Reports* and other buying guides. Read some general information that will enhance your knowledge of a product.

I do this before a major purchase, and it always pays off. Three years ago, I saved $2,700 on the purchase of a new $10,000 car because I spent a couple of hours in the library reading about the car and its dealer costs. Many people, giving in to the salesperson, would have paid close to the sticker price.

Keep yourself informed. Walk away if you are confused, feel pressured, or feel you are making an impulse buying decision. As you make better decisions, you will find it much less of a chore and much more fun than you thought to take control of your financial destiny.

Estate Planning Simplified

Everyone should have an updated will to protect them from the possibility of their estate going to probate. No one wants the state to decide how their property is divided up. Another alternative to a will is setting up a family trust. A trust is a great way to pass on your estate to your heirs. Trusts are much better than wills because they are more detailed and harder to contest. You also can change beneficiaries at any time.

For most people, a revocable living trust is the best route to go. It's a painless way to pass on your estate, and you can revoke the trust if you feel it's not up to your expectations. You have complete authority when you are alive, and you choose the trustee who will distribute your estate when you die.

If you want your spouse to have steady income when you die, and then have the trust distributed when he or she dies, consider a QTIP (qualified terminable interest property trust). Sounds scary, but it's not that complex. The trust is managed by the surviving spouse and the trustee. The surviving spouse gets income from the trust and can sometimes even get a portion of the principal. The surviving spouse cannot change the beneficiaries who will receive all the assets from the trust after he or she dies. You should review trusts every couple of years to make sure they include all your assets. Also consider a pre-nuptial agreement before you get married so you can get around strict state laws that dictate how your estate will be distributed. If you are already married, use a post-nuptial agreement to accomplish this task. The key to either agreement being successful between the parties is complete honesty and understanding of the reasons for the agreement.

At the very minimum, make sure you have an updated will to at least give you some protection. If you get a trust, you still need a will that makes provisions for any assets the trust may have excluded. Ask friends and relatives if they know a good estate lawyer to help you get started.

Sticky Inheritance

Here's a great trick to avoid inheritance disputes when the time arrives. Mark as many valuables as you can with color-coded stickers designating who the items will go to. Apply the stickers in a place where they will not be seen, such as the underside of a chair or bottom of a vase. Include items that don't have a lot of value. The little things can sometimes be the most confusing for heirs to divide. You don't need to inform your relatives about the marking of these items if you don't want to put them in an awkward or embarrassing position. Just make sure that your wishes are clearly spelled out in your will.

Mr. Postman's Mistake

Slow mail delivery can cost you money in unexpected interest charges and late payment fees on credit cards. In your checkbook, note dates that you sent checks. If your check arrives late and you are not habitually late, the company most likely will waive penalty payments if you tell them the exact day you sent the check. Also, be aware of dates that the bill comes in the mail. If the bill comes late, call the company immediately and tell them about the bill's arrival. The company may allow a grace period on your account if it knows the bill arrived late.

Squeeze Extra Money Out of Your Bank

You can choose from many bank services and products these days. These few pointers may help you squeeze a few more dollars out of your banker:

- Don't pay unnecessary service charges at your bank. Fees vary since deregulation has occurred. Call your bank and find out the fees on your accounts. Then call around to other banks in the area to see if your bank is competitive. If you approach your current bank and say you're going to take your business elsewhere, the bank may lower or eliminate excess fees altogether. Don't be intimidated by the banker's nice suit and big office.

- Never let money pile up in non-interest-bearing accounts such as checking accounts. Have your money working for you at all times. Most interest-bearing accounts have minimum balance requirements.

- Set up a money market mutual fund account rather than a bank savings account. You'll get a higher rate of return on your savings. Most money market mutual funds offer a small book of checks if you need to redeem shares.

- Make regular deposits in the money market mutual fund and use this money as your emergency fund. I recommend that you accumulate at least three months income in this account. If you have excess money building up in your checking account, transfer this money over to your money market. When you have more money in your money market than necessary, look into a six-month or one-year CD or short-term government security.

- Take advantage of no-fee checking accounts and other service packages. These packages quite often include safe deposit boxes, free traveler's checks, and more. Senior citizens should look for banks that cater specifically to their needs. Check out qualifications for fees associated with different balances in your accounts.

A Lend Could End a Friendship

This advice may sound negative and cold, but you should never lend money to a friend. (Of course you may have an emotional situation when you need to override this rule.) If you do decide to lend money to a buddy, be prepared for the worst. Nine times out of ten you don't get paid back, and this problem could seriously jeopardize your relationship. Look at the situation this way: If your friend can't get the money through traditional sources, you can bet you are making a high-risk loan. Just say no.

Separate or Joint Accounts?

Should you and your spouse have separate bank accounts if one of you has poor credit? If you don't have poor credit, most couples feel it is best to put all their funds into one pot and try to work things out over time. This strategy may not be the best if either spouse has bad credit. If you are dealing with this problem, consider splitting up your accounts until you have all your debt under control. Otherwise, with the joint account, you are both held liable for any debts that only one of you has. This circumstance may or may not be a problem depending on how you both handle your finances. Don't forget that money problems are the number one concern facing marriages.

Having separate credit situations can be advantageous if you want to get a loan or a credit card for both of you. All you need to do is use the spouse's name who has the best credit history to get the loan.

Joint Bank Account Hassles

Be careful of joint bank accounts because they can trigger some inheritance problems. Too often the surviving spouse treats adult children equally in a will but puts one child on bank accounts for bill paying if the parent becomes incapacitated. Upon the parent's death, the joint-owner child becomes sole owner of the parent's accounts, contrary to the parent's intent. Even if the joint-owner child shares the money with the other siblings, there is still a gift tax consequence. To avoid this problem, sign a durable power of attorney and make one or more children agents to sign. Leave the bank account in the parent's name and write the will to divide the account equally. Remember, if you only have a will, your estate will go through probate proceedings.

Don't Use Automatic Debits

Avoid making any kind of purchase via a monthly automatic charge on your credit card or through your bank account. By letting a company debit your account, you take financial control away from yourself. In addition, you are setting yourself up for problems if you ever want to cancel or change these options. Quite often, the company debiting the amount takes too much money, fails to comply with a cancel request, or gets your account confused with another. If you do experience problems, automatic debits are very difficult to void. Also, many companies are experiencing fraud problems among their employees. These employees swipe numbers on cards and accounts and might just charge a night out on the town or worse.

Check Mate

I used to hate having to pay my bank $12 for new checks. I got 200 individual checks that look like they came from a prison—blue and boring. For a cheaper check option, contact Current Check Products, P.O. Box 19000, Colorado Springs, CO 80935. Phone (800) 533-3973. Ask for a color brochure of check choices. Not only are the checks half the price of most banks, but they have some great designs, like the Elvis edition, animals, and landscape scenes. My favorite is the check that looks like a dollar bill. Another good company is Checks in the Mail, Inc. at (800) 733-4443. If you are looking for business checks, you can save even more because banks charge businesses more than individuals. Why are these check companies cheaper? There's no bank as the middleman.

Safe Deposit Box No-Nos

Be careful about putting cash, savings bonds, and stock certificates in your safe deposit box. Theft is on the rise in metropolitan area banks, and they are not as well protected from safe deposit box robbers as they used to be. Many robbers are forging keys and scurrying off with the loot. If a robber does get you, you'll have a hard time proving that you had any of these negotiable currencies in your box. Invest in a sturdy, fireproof safe, and tuck it away in an unlikely place at home. If you're concerned about having valuables at home, make copies of all negotiable documents and put them in your safe deposit box. Having a backup never hurts.

Cash Gobblers

If you deposit cash into an ATM machine, watch out. The receipt you receive from the machine is not valid proof you made the deposit. Most machines do not know how much money you place in the envelope. If the teller makes an oversight opening the envelope for final deposit, you are at the mercy of human error. Deposit your cash at the teller's station inside the bank where a valid receipt is proof of deposit. This advice applies to cash deposits only. If you deposit checks in an ATM, you are safe. Also, if you use the ATM often, make sure you use only machines that are associated with your bank so you don't have to pay transaction fees.

Lose the Bank Blues

Deposit your paycheck with direct deposit if your employer allows it. Not only do you save the time and inconvenience of going to the ATM machine every two weeks, but the money becomes "good funds" faster. Most companies that have direct deposit also allow you to send a portion of each paycheck to an investment vehicle of your choosing. This is a great way to begin to save.

How to Encourage Your Kids to Be $ensible $avers

Because the financial world is getting more and more complex, we all should be looking at ways to better prepare the youth of today to handle financial matters. Whatever their ages, start to teach your kids smart money moves.

Make sure your children get a regular allowance. Some people say you should start this routine at age 6 or 7. Maybe $2.50 every week. Of course you need to raise the amount as the kids get older. The allowance is a great way to teach a child the value of money.

When your children are age 10 or so, open a savings account for them and match whatever they sock away in that account. This practice is a great incentive. Suggest to your child that it may be a good idea to put a birthday check or Christmas check in the account occasionally.

Talk to your child about the importance of being disciplined with savings and the rewards it brings. If you think through some ideas, you can come up with creative ways to teach children savings habits. I remember my father encouraging me to save for a three-wheel trike when I was very young. I religiously saved pennies, dimes, and quarters for a long time. My father kept tabs on my results and was quite impressed. He rewarded me with a new trike for my birthday and let me spend the money I had saved at the local amusement park. This experience taught me about the unknown rewards that can come with saving.

When children are between the ages of 14 and 16, suggest the possibility of a part-time job to help pay for some of their social expenses. When kids realize they can make a lot more money than their puny allowance, they usually make the sacrifice. A good summer job can help the child develop good work habits and teach them what it's like to sweat for a buck.

When college comes around, encourage your student to share in some of the financial burdens. Make your child responsible for books or social expenses. This lesson may lead to a better understanding of the value in higher education.

By using painless ways to teach children the basics of personal finance, you are preparing them to handle life's money curve balls when they're older.

ACTION LIST:

1. If you are not currently investing in no-load mutual funds, consider putting at least some savings into them. Contact a mutual fund family to receive performance results and a prospectus.

    Date completed: _____

2. If you insist on investing in individual stocks, review your performance and make sure you aren't taking any heavy losses waiting for a stock to rebound.

    Date completed: _____

3. Invest in bonds if you want steady income or want to diversify your portfolio to a greater extent.

    Date completed: _____

4. Your investment advisor should be an important ally in your financial plan. Make sure he or she is not excessively charging fees and commissions to your account.

    Date completed: _____

CHAPTER 15

The Tax Man Cometh

> Washington is a place where politicians don't know which
> way is up and consequently taxes don't know which way is
> down.
>
> —Robert Orben

Slash Your Tax Bill Starting Today

Tax time always seems to be lurking over our shoulders. To help reduce the stress associated with tax season, pay attention to tax issues throughout the year. In this chapter, I share with you several tax-saving ideas that could save you hundreds of dollars come April 15. These tips are important because the average American now pays about 40% of gross income in all forms of taxes including federal, state and local, sales, and property. It's time to fight back.

Obviously, you want to keep as much money in your pocket as possible, without paying Uncle Sam any more than necessary. You still have to pay taxes but forearmed with some basic knowledge of IRS rules, you can save yourself a bundle on taxes.

Retirement Plans

First, invest in every tax-deductible retirement plan that you have available to you. You can double the power of your year-end bonus by putting it into an IRA, 401(k) plan, or a similar tax-deductible and tax-deferred savings program. Start with whatever plan you have that is tax-deductible. Invest as much as possible in this account. If your employer offers any matching funds, don't say no to a free lunch. If you invest now, you are spending money on your future financial security, and you won't need to pay any more taxes than necessary on your additional pay.

Kiddie Deductions

You can legally double the tax deduction on your kids by putting them to work in your part-time or full-time business and paying them a salary. You can keep the dependency exemption and also take an employee salary deduction with your business. The kids can do a lot of things like filing, stuffing envelopes, stapling, cleaning the office, etc.

Timing Your Investments

Make sure you are purchasing your investments at the right time of the year. For instance, it's a good idea to purchase stocks and mutual funds the day after dividends are declared and distributed. If you buy before distribution, the value of your investment drops by the amount of the distribution, and then you are responsible for taxes already (Uncle Sam gets you somehow). Always *sell* just before dividends are distributed to get a better share price.

Charity Deductions

The IRS is nice enough to give you a deduction of 12 cents for every mile that you drive to and from charity work. If you do a lot of work for your church or the local shelter, don't overlook this great deduction.

If you want to give away an asset to a charity, donate an asset that has gained in value. You avoid the capital gains tax and can deduct the entire value of the asset you have given. If you have an asset that has lost value, sell the asset, use the loss to offset any other capital gains, then give a cash contribution and take the charitable deduction.

Travel Deductions

You can take a tax deduction by setting up a job interview in the region you are planning to take a vacation to. As long as the job interview is for a position in the same field you now work in, the cost of the trip is fully tax-deductible. The deduction includes airfare, rental car, and passport fees.

Property Tax Deductions

If you are fed up with rising property taxes, contact your local tax assessor's office to get information about these deductible areas you may fall into:

- The "Homestead exemption" could cut about 20% off your bill.

- A personal property tax exemption could enable you to deduct "necessary household items" such as a washer and dryer or refrigerator.

- The veterans exemption of up to $50 per year is available to veterans.

- You can take a home-business exemption if you operate a business from home.

- A senior citizens exemption is available to people 65 or older.

You can appeal your property tax assessment if you feel it is unfair or in error. You may be paying too much.

Put Old Clothes to Work

If you donate your old clothes to charity, you can save at least $50 on your 1996 taxes. You may not think those old suits and dresses stashed in your closet are worth much, but the IRS does, if you value them properly. Generally, you can value old clothes at about 10% to 25% less than you bought them for if they are in decent shape. The staff at your local Goodwill donation center usually can help you get a handle on how much your donation is worth. Insist on a receipt for your records. You need to be able to back up how much you claim because the IRS requires documentation of your charitable donations.

Kiddie Care

Child-care credits are available on your tax return for expenses beyond just day care. Payments to nurseries and kindergartens are included in this credit. You cannot include payments beyond kindergarten unless they pertain to child care rather than education.

Dependent Deduction

If you and other family members are supporting a dependent in your household, decide early in the year who should claim the dependent on his or her taxes. To deduct the dependent's medical expenses, that person must pay the medical bills and claim the dependent on his or her tax return. If you and your siblings jointly support the dependent and none of you pays more than half the support, you can file a multiple support agreement and get a dependency exemption.

A Gift from the IRS

If you have bought a house in the last few years, you may save some big bucks on taxes. The IRS recently ruled that seller-paid points can be deducted for house purchases made after December 31, 1990. Previously, only points that you, the buyer, paid could be deducted. The IRS looks at these points as an adjustment to the cost of the home on the buyer's part.

If you are entitled to a claim for deductions in any previous years, just file an amended return on form 1040X, which you can get at your local IRS office. In the top right corner, write *seller-paid points*. You need to attach a copy of your settlement statement with the amended return. Make sure you remember this deduction; you could get back several hundred dollars.

IRA Deductions

With all the confusing rules these days, you may not be sure if you're able to deduct your IRA contribution (information on how to determine deductibilty is contained in Chapter 16). Don't be discouraged if you cannot deduct your IRA contribution this year. When you put money into an IRA, the money still compounds tax-deferred until you withdraw funds. At that point, you will owe taxes on only the investment returns, or income you have received over the years. You will not need to pay taxes on the principal invested. You must keep accurate records of all deductions taken and report non-deductible IRA contributions on IRS Form 8606. When you withdraw funds in the future, you will have all the tax information on hand to easily determine your taxable portion. Keep socking that money away.

Check Those Tax Shelters

Because of new rules and tighter controls over tax shelter promoters, be sure you review all offering circulars with a tax advisor before investing in any tax shelter. The IRS may disallow tax shelter losses if you cannot demonstrate an economic profit motive for the investment besides tax savings. Tax shelter promoters must also register the tax shelters they organize with the IRS and provide the registration number to investors. Investors are required to report the number on their personal return. Failure to do so can result in a $250 penalty. Also, deductions for tax shelter partnerships are limited under the new laws.

Commonly Overlooked Deductions

When preparing your taxes, determine whether you qualify for any of these commonly overlooked deductions:

- Tax preparation fees
- Safe deposit box fees
- 25% deduction for self-employed health insurance
- Subscriptions to investment or trade newsletters (yes, *The $ensible $aver* book and newsletter are included)
- IRA trustee fees
- Moving expenses to a new job

Don't waste your money filing electronically; you speed up your refund only by a week or two. Also, make sure you are using the correct filing status; it could save you as much as 20%. Check with your tax preparer or accountant if you have any further questions, or consult *J.K. Lasser's Your Income Tax* manual, found at any bookstore.

Prepare Your Taxes Yourself and Save

No matter how much money you have, preparing your own taxes is the best way to save money. I'm not talking just about the cost of paying a tax preparer, but also the cost associated with the missed deductions and mistakes that many preparers make.

Every year *Money* magazine has a contest for tax preparers all over the country. The magazine gives about 25 preparers an income tax scenario for an average American family. Surprisingly, only a few came within $1,000 of the amount to be refunded to the taxpayer or paid to the IRS. Most preparers were thousands off! I don't think that anyone doing his or her own taxes could do much worse. As a matter of fact, I am certain you can do much better because only you know the ins and outs of your financial situation.

If you don't do any of your taxes now, I suggest you do them at least for one or two years so you can get a feel of your tax picture. The advantage is that you can catch more deductions, which may save you hundreds or even thousands. You also have the added advantage of being totally prepared for next year's tax planning.

Many people feel intimidated by taxes when preparation time rolls around. They think the numbers and calculations involved are too complex to handle themselves.

I have done my own taxes since I started filing 12 years ago. I finished my returns and sent them to the IRS on February 5 this year. I spent a total of 7 hours completing all the paperwork, and I know that I saved at least $30 per hour for the cost of a preparer. Granted, I'm pretty well organized with papers and receipts properly filed, but that's because I have been prepared in previous years. Tax planning throughout the year is vital. I also have the added peace of mind that my return is correct and that I maximized all my available deductions.

Try preparing your own taxes for a year or two. I can almost guarantee you will be frustrated at first, but the process gets easier as the years pass. If you get stumped or just can't go on, you can still call your preparer.

The IRS has a number of free publications that can help you do your own taxes and a toll-free information line to answer your questions: 1-800-829-4477. Again, I also recommend *J.K. Lasser's Your Income Tax* manual, which you can purchase at any bookstore. This excellent publication has been a godsend for me.

What Are Your Chances of Getting Audited?

For the first time in many years, the odds of being audited have actually gone up. And the odds probably will increase even more in the future.

In 1995, wage earners with incomes less than $100,000 were audited at the rate of only 1%. Those with higher incomes could expect to get audited at the rate of about 5%.

The self-employed with gross receipts over $100,000 were looking at an audit rate of about 4%. Farmers with receipts over the $100,000 mark had about a 2% chance of getting the IRS on their backs. Finally, corporations with receipts less than $1,000,000 were audited at the rate of about 4%.

On an overall basis, considering all taxpayers at different levels, the audit rate averaged out to an amazingly low .85 percent.

These rates will change soon. The IRS has invested in new computer equipment that will enable the service to almost double the amount of audits it now performs. As many as two million taxpayers will be affected with a reported income boost to the government of $10 billion a year. In addition, the IRS will be conducting more "live" audits because of new legislation putting more auditors out in the field.

If some of your deductions have been shaky, or you think that you may have under-reported income in the past few years, you had better go back and make sure everything is square.

The table on the following page shows 1995 data pertaining to your chances of getting audited. The data includes all field audits and office audits performed. For 1995, the IRS reviewed 1,058,966 individual tax returns. This number is a slight increase over the number of returns audited in 1994. The big news is that audit percentages for Schedule C filers (self-employed) increased in all income categories.

1995 Percentage of Returns Audited

Individuals (Non-Business)**	1995
Under $25,000	.71%
$25,000 to $50,000	.58
$50,000 to $100,000	.88
$100,000 and over	4.03

** The overall U.S. average for all individuals is .85%

continued

Self-Employed (Schedule C)

Under $25,000	2.24%
$25,000 to $100,000	2.41
$100,000 and over	3.91

Farmers (Schedule F)

Under $100,000	1.06%
$100,000 and over	2.06%

Partnerships

All income categories	.61%

Corporations (Assets)

Under $250,000	1.33%
$250,000 to $1 million	3.94
$1 million to $5 million	9.35
$5 million to $10 million	19.04
$10 million to $50 million	23.31
$50 million to $100 million	25.56
$100 million to $250 million	31.15
$250 million and over	52.11

What Uncle Sam Is Looking For

The IRS looks for certain items when processing your tax return. These items are known as *red flags*. If the IRS encounters one or more red flags, it may bounce your 1040 form and return it to you for an audit. Don't be a statistic. The following sections describe some of the items that draw the attention of the tax man.

Home Office Deductions

This area is one of Uncle Sam's favorite targets. The IRS has gone to court repeatedly, winning support for its tough stand on rejecting taxpayers' deductions.

To take a deduction on part of your home, or to deduct a portion of your rent for the space you use as a home office, you must satisfy several requirements. You must be able to prove that you use the room regularly and exclusively for business. This room must be the principal place of your business. Using the space to meet with customers is acceptable. Your deductions probably won't hold up if you take work home from a primary place of employment or if your office doubles as the family room.

Travel and Entertainment

Entertaining prospective customers often is necessary to win their business. However, the IRS knows that many people tuck their personal bills in with their business receipts. They estimate lost revenues of about $1.5 billion due to this practice. No small potatoes. You can write off only 50% of the cost of business meals and entertainment. Keep organized and documented receipts and a diary stating the business purpose of all receipts.

Personal Interest

The Tax Reform Act of 1986 introduced several sets of rules for interest write-offs. The most favorable rules are those for home mortgage interest, which is generally 100% deductible.

Another group of regulations limits the allowable deduction for interest on funds borrowed for investment purposes (such as margin accounts used to buy securities). Investment interest is deductible only to the extent it is matched by investment income, a category that includes interest, dividends, and capital gains (subject to restrictions).

The toughest rules prohibit any deduction on Schedule A of form 1040 for interest paid on personal or "consumer" loans. This grouping includes credit card and charge account debts, college fees, auto loans, and overdue income taxes.

The IRS suspects that many taxpayers misclassify their interest deductions. For example, if you incur margin interest on a brokerage account and then buy a car, you cannot claim your margin interest as a deduction. If you have a sideline business and properly file a Schedule C for the self-employed, you cannot deduct interest on a personal debt as a business expense. The same goes for a farmer who files a Schedule F tax form.

Although you want to deduct everything you can, be careful to avoid these audit triggers:

- Failure to pay self-employment taxes
- Questionable hobby deductions
- Off-the-record babysitters
- Excessive home-office deduction
- Excessive IRA deductions

How to Deal with the Tax Man

When confronting tax issues, many taxpayers choose to deal with the IRS directly instead of using an accountant or lawyer. These quick tips can help you deal with the IRS:

- Be very organized and have all information summarized whenever you dispute any item on your tax return. Have all your calculations written down so the IRS can see them clearly. Being organized shows the IRS you are in control of your finances.

- Be very businesslike with the IRS. Most IRS employees have seen it all and just want to hear the facts. Showing representatives you have a great personality by telling a good joke will not win their affection. In fact, it may annoy them.

- Get involved in only basic tax matters. If you show up at an IRS audit wanting to discuss a matter relating to depreciation but don't know what you're talking about, you can end up looking pretty stupid. Seek out a competent professional if you think you are in too deep.

- Above all, be totally forthright and honest in your assessment of any tax situation. Don't try to cover up the lack of documentation or a certain problem area. Again, the IRS has seen it all, and anything you do that is out of the ordinary can arouse suspicion and get them on your back. The best bet is to always have proper documentation for any tax problem you may have. Remember, "Just the facts, ma'am."

If you are called to an IRS office audit, the IRS is usually just checking to make sure deductions claimed have proper supporting documentation. Don't be alarmed when you get a letter for this type of audit. The audit usually doesn't involve extensive legal or technical matters. If you have the appropriate papers, you have nothing to be concerned about.

Field audits are a different story. The IRS usually asks for a field audit if you have discrepancies and questions on your tax return. Most field audits are performed on medium-size businesses or individuals who have part-time income from a small business. These audits often involve many technical and legal issues and should not be approached lightly. Seek the counsel of a good tax advisor. If the situation is complicated, ask to have the advisor with you at a field audit.

Computer Spying?

The IRS has been developing a computer system that will give it better access to private databases to call up profiles on taxpayers. The IRS says this system is only a research project and it will not infringe on Americans' right to privacy. However, many Capitol Hill insiders are nervous about this new system.

They say they want to access a wide variety of information to expand their ability to collect $100 billion in unpaid taxes and catch non-compliers. The new system will have access to commercial lending sources, state and local licensing authorities, construction contracts, currency and banking reports, financial transactions from state and local governments, and information on significant financial transactions in newspapers or the media.

It seems pretty obvious to many in Washington that the IRS is trying to get its foot in the door to track down detailed data about taxpayers in general, not just those who have "unpaid" taxes. If the IRS gets this detailed system up and running, what's to stop them from checking privileged personal information?

Don't Overpay Your Taxes: Adjust Your W–4

Don't let the IRS take your hard-earned cash and make money off it. If you are getting a refund from the Fed this year, you're admitting you are a poor tax planner. Many Americans use their tax refunds to help pay bills! Does it make sense to give the IRS a $1,000 or $2,000 interest-free loan every year?

I was on a radio show recently and was told by a CPA that he saw nothing wrong with people getting refunds because it was the only way they could save. I was ready to explode but instead asked the man to give me $100 every two weeks, and I would gladly give him back his money at the end of the year. With no interest, of course.

He thought I was nutty, but is it any crazier to give the money to the IRS? With this type of irrational advice from the so-called *money experts,* it's no surprise that only about 5% of this country saves religiously. If you are getting a refund this year, please, please, take it down to the bank and save it for a rainy day. Then go directly to your human resources office at work and ask for help to rework your W–4 statement. The more allowances you claim, the less money will be taken from your paycheck. Take this cash and add it to your savings nest egg.

Make Tax Bill Copies

When paying any type of taxes, always keep copies of the check and information that you send with your payment in case your payment gets lost in the red tape. If you don't have proof of the payment or the proper documentation, there will be a tremendous amount of confusion between you and the tax service. Also, when you send payments or documents, send them registered mail so you know they will get there. It's not uncommon for the IRS to never receive payment from individuals due to mailing mistakes.

ACTION LIST:

1. Get out last year's tax return and review whether you took all the deductions you could have. Use this chapter as a guide to help you pinpoint missed deductions. Make a note of any deductions you may want to take for next year's return.

    Date completed: _____

2. If you don't currently prepare your taxes yourself, make an effort to do so for at least a year or two. You will gain new-found knowledge about your taxes.

    Date completed: _____

3. To reduce your chances of getting audited, pay special attention to red flags discussed in this chapter. If you avoid these common mistakes on your return, the IRS will be much less likely to audit you.

    Date completed: _____ .

CHAPTER 16

A Retirement of Luxury

> *There comes a time in everyone's life when they realize they have to plan for their financial future. Those who realize this at an early age are well set for a life of stability and financial freedom.*
>
> —*Mark W. Miller*

Picture this: You are finally retired and are walking down a white sand beach. The cool sand moves between your toes, feeling like a gentle massage. The sun is setting and you spot seagulls across the horizon while a slight breeze brushes your face. The waves make a sound that almost lulls you to sleep. Ah, paradise.

You turn around and look at your footprints that are left behind, and you see a big cane hole next to them!

Is this retirement? I sure hope the beach part is, but the cane hole doesn't need to be there. More and more, smart savers are realizing that by planning when they're younger, it is possible to retire and live in style before you are 65. You can use several ways to get to a comfortable retirement. Read on.

Tax-Deferred Plans

A vital step toward retirement is to take full advantage of any tax-deferred retirement plans available to you. These plans are the most powerful way to build wealth because all monies invested work for you tax-free. Retirement plans offer two key benefits: Your contribution is tax-deductible, and the money in the accounts accumulates interest and capital gains on a tax-free basis until you withdraw it.

If your employer offers a 401(k) plan or SEP (simplified employee plan), contribute the maximum amount. If you are a teacher and have access to a 403(b) plan, contribute the most you can. By contributing the maximum allowed per year, you can accumulate enough money for a great lifestyle when you retire.

You also should use your IRA (individual retirement account) as a safe haven for retirement funds. Even if you are covered by a qualified plan at work, continue to make nondeductible contributions to your IRA. Contributing the maximum to all plans is a sure way to have plenty of money when you retire. Each plan is described in detail later in this chapter.

Contribute to your plan today, not in two or three years. If you invested just $2,000 per year between the ages of 20 and 25 and never invested another penny, you will have more money at age 65 than if you started at age 25 and invested $2,000 for the next 20 years at the same rate of return! If you have college-age children or grandchildren, why not help them get started with an IRA to teach them a lesson or two about saving?

The following table shows you the results if you invested $4,000 per year in a retirement plan. The first column indicates the age at which you begin contributing.

If you have 10 or more years until retirement and have control over your plan, I suggest that you invest in equity securities because they will outperform other investments in the long run. A no-load mutual fund is an excellent option. Good company plans give you options for investing as well. Choose the option that provides a good return on your money over time. Don't get caught up in outstanding short-term gains. Also, investing in an account paying 4% or 5% is not going to make you wealthy over the years.

If you need to contribute more to obtain your retirement goals, try to work it out. Retirement years are when you need money the most and hopefully will be able to enjoy it. By planning properly and

$4,000 Investment Per Year before Taxes*

Present Age	Contribution Acquired at Age 65
20	$6,088,871
25	3,440,570
30	1,937,852
35	1,085,170
40	601,336
45	362,795
50	171,013
55	82,618
60	32,461

*12% compounded annually in tax-free retirement plans

using all your available investment resources, you can see that early retirement is not an impossibility.

A Quick Lesson on IRAs

Here are some general tips about IRAs:

- You may contribute up to $2,000 of your earned income to an IRA each year until you become age 70½, when withdrawals become mandatory. Earnings during this period of time are tax-deferred until withdrawn. A 10% penalty is assessed for any withdrawals before age 59½.

- You may deduct your full IRA contribution if neither you nor your spouse is covered by a qualified pension plan, or if your income is under $25,000 and you are married and filing a joint return. A limited deduction is available if your income is not more than $10,000 above that amount. If you're covered by a qualified pension plan, you get no deduction whatsoever if your income is above $35,000 and you are married filing jointly.

- If you make nondeductible IRA contributions, you must file form 8606 each year you make contributions or withdraw any amounts from your IRA. The total nondeductible amount is your IRA basis, which is not taxed when withdrawn. You need not segregate deductible and nondeductible investments, because your basis computation applies to the total value of all your IRAs when withdrawals happen.

After explaining these rules, I realize how the government has turned the IRA into a big hassle. When the concept of the IRA was first introduced, it was a simple approach designed to help people save, so they could augment the inadequate Social Security system. Now IRAs are a legal mumbo-jumbo mess. Still, despite all the rules and regulations and dumb accounting tricks, an IRA plus company plans is about all we have to help us toward our goal of retirement. I just wish that Congress would catch a clue and try one easy method: Keep it simple.

When Should You Start Planning for Your Golden Years?

There's really no specific time or date when you should start saving for retirement. You need to evaluate how much money you have now, what Social Security and pensions you will receive, and what kind of lifestyle you want to have when you retire. Some people get concerned about retirement when they are in their 20s, which gives them a tremendous leg up. Others don't start to realize the importance of retirement savings until retirement is just 10 years around the corner. For every dollar you set aside at age 35, you will need about three dollars at the age 55 to have the same effect. The advantage to starting young is that you can set up a plan to build upon for many years to come.

If you have been unable to save for your retirement, try to start saving at least 15 years before the date you plan to retire. A more conservative outlook gives you about 25 years. A retirement date for most people is probably around age 65, but the sooner you start, the earlier you can retire. Retiring early is everyone's dream, but that may be impossible if you wait until the last hour to sock money away.

Realistically, most Americans begin their disciplined retirement saving in their 40s. You should then be adding to these savings amounts in your 50s, when the responsibilities of the household are not such a burden. Your kids probably have moved out of the house and their college expenses have been paid.

Take a long-term approach when investing for retirement. The best long-term growth comes in the stock market, so you should be exploring conservative stocks and mutual funds. Your return over the years will determine whether you have a long, worry-free, and fulfilling retirement. As I have written, max out your pension plans or 401(k)s at work and any IRAs or SEPs that you have available.

All these plans can be tax-deductible or provide before-tax investing, and the best ones enable you to make the investment choices yourself. Don't buy the argument that you shouldn't contribute to a retirement plan if you cannot deduct the money. Your money still grows tax-free until you withdraw it at retirement.

By all means, don't put all your investment eggs in one basket, and as you get closer to retirement age, make sure you can take out the eggs easily without harming your investment performance. View your retirement portfolio as an ongoing financial plan, because when you retire, you are not at the finish line. Life can go on for many years after retirement, and a good plan must be in place for you to live comfortably.

Don't forget your home, which can be an important asset when you retire. Your home possesses valuable tax advantages as the years go by. If you plan on staying in a house a long time and paying off the mortgage, make sure the house has great investment value. Then you can sell your home for a substantial profit, and sell it fast, come retirement time. If the house is not a good value, it will be a burden at retirement and only tie up important assets.

Take time out today and begin to explore your retirement options. What kind of lifestyle do you want to live? How much money will it take to achieve this goal? While some may think that they need a million dollars to retire, others may think that is not nearly enough. The amount needed for your comfortable retirement has to be determined by you only. Take into account the fact that inflation has averaged about 4% over the last several decades and will eat away at your retirement nest egg. A million dollars now won't be worth the same when you retire.

Bullet-Proof Your Lifetime Savings

When was the last time your boss, or anyone, said to you, "Let's sit down and make sure you are saving enough for retirement."

Making your retirement nest egg grow is your responsibility alone, but I'm here to give a little help.

As stated earlier, the best way to save for retirement is through tax-advantaged retirement vehicles such as a 401(k), 403(b), IRA, Keogh, or SEP-IRA. The power of tax-deferred savings is unparalleled. I want to give you some more detailed information about these plans so you can see if you qualify for any of them.

If you take one penny and double it every day, you will have $10,747,000 after 31 days. Do the math, because it's pretty amazing. If Uncle Sam comes along on the fifth day and tells you that you need to pay him taxes on 28% of your savings, he'll take a good chunk of your money. This tax eats into the compounding effect. If Uncle Sam comes back and asks for more money on days 10, 15, 20, 25, and 30, your money will be worth only $1,500,000. You would lose about $9 million! Who wants an uncle who does that to you? Now do you understand the importance of tax-deferred savings?

If you already contribute religiously to a retirement plan at work, you're doing well. Other options are available to help bullet-proof your retirement plan. Take a look at the following sections and see if you can invest in any of these plans as an extra bonus to what you have now.

IRA

You establish an IRA on your own, decide how much to contribute, and make all the investment decisions yourself. Contributions may be tax-deductible depending on your situation, as discussed earlier in this chapter. All money grows tax-deferred. Your maximum contribution is $2,000 per year for an individual or $2,250 for you and a non-working spouse. The fees usually run about $15 to $20 per year to open an account. A fully funded IRA is the cornerstone of your nest egg if contributions are fully deductible. If your contributions are nondeductible, fund other plans instead.

401(k) and 403(b)

You contribute part of your salary to these plans. Your employer also has the option of contributing. You make these contributions before taxes are taken out, and your money grows tax-deferred. The maximum contribution is $9,240 a year. You cannot beat the advantages to these plans, especially if your employer matches funds. Sometimes the plans are limited by your employers' investment choices, which is the price you pay for the benefit.

SEP-IRA (Simplified Employee Plan)

A SEP-IRA is similar to an IRA, but it doesn't have all the restrictions. SEP-IRA is an option if you have any self-employment income. All contributions are fully deductible, and your money grows tax-deferred. You can contribute up to 15% of your earnings and a maximum of $30,000 per year. The cost is generally about $30 annually. A SEP-IRA is a simple way to contribute the maximum to a retirement plan. You can use this plan in addition to other investment plans.

Keogh

This plan is available if you have any self-employment income. Keoghs enable you to contribute the highest percentage of your income of any plan. All contributions are deductible, and your money grows tax-deferred. You can contribute 15% to 25% of your self-employment income up to $30,000. Most Keoghs cost less than $75 annually. You receive the same benefits of a SEP, but a Keogh requires considerably more paperwork that you must file with the IRS. A Keogh is the best plan if you want to contribute more than 15% of your income.

Annuity Power

One of the best and safest tax shelters after your company plan or IRA is the variable annuity. A variable annuity is a product developed by insurance companies that enables you to save money tax-free for retirement purposes. An annuity is almost like a tax-sheltered mutual fund purchase. When you put your money into a variable annuity, the money compounds tax-free until you withdraw it.

Annuities originated in the 1950s after insurance companies successfully lobbied Congress that the country needed a savings plan that was free of taxes so Americans wouldn't retire broke. No laws at the time allowed this program, but because of the insurance industry's financial pull, they were able to offer annuities. Today's IRA is nothing but a high-bred annuity.

For years, most annuities were fixed; you put in a certain amount and when the annuity matured, you received a certain amount back. With new product demands came a much better version of the annuity called the variable annuity. The key advantage to this plan is that you have control over the investment choices of your annuity. You don't just give your money to the insurance company, who quotes you a fixed rate you will get on your money.

Most variable annuities have investment choices consisting of different mutual fund families. You can pick and choose the funds you want to be in and can move from fund to fund at no charge. You can achieve a good investment mix this way, and you obviously can achieve substantial returns on your money—much higher than the usual rates with fixed annuities.

Although annuities are great investment options, you should use them only after you have exhausted all company and individual plans to their fullest. The money you invest in an IRA, Keogh, or SEP-IRA is tax-deductible whereas only the investment earnings in an annuity are tax-deferred. You have already paid taxes on money invested in an annuity.

One advantage to annuities is that they have no legal requirements when you must start distributions. Plan on keeping your money in the annuity for at least seven years, though, because most companies levy stiff withdrawal penalties in the early years. Make sure you have no commissions or loads up front. Remember, you are investing long-term retirement money.

When the time comes to withdraw money, don't ever annuitize your annuity. This means that the company keeps the balance in the annuity and pays you guaranteed income for a set period. Sounds great, but the tables are always tipped in the company's direction when you annuitize. The company wouldn't be in business unless it operated this way.

Variable annuities are popping up all over the place today. Some of the larger mutual fund families are offering them. Check with Fidelity Investments (800-544-8888) or Vanguard (800-851-4999). The variable annuity can be an excellent tool in your investment workshop.

Your Age Is Your Gauge

When it comes to figuring the right mix of equities (stocks) and fixed-income securities (bonds, CDs, etc.) in your retirement portfolio, use your age as your guide. The farther away from retirement you are, the higher percentage you should invest in equities. The closer you are to retirement, the more you should invest in fixed-income securities. As a rule, 100 minus your age is the amount you should invest in equities. As an example, if you are 55, you should put 45% of your nest egg in equities. The other 55% goes into fixed-income investments such as bonds. Adjust your percentages every five years.

Are You Fully Covered?

Your retirement nest egg may not be fully covered by the FDIC (Federal Deposit Insurance Corporation). The maximum covered limit for bank deposits of IRAs, Keoghs, and 401(k)s is $100,000 combined ($100,000 per bank).

If you have $85,000 in an IRA and $90,000 in a Keogh account at the same bank, the FDIC insures only $100,000 of your entire savings. That leaves a whopping $75,000 uninsured. The system operates just like a normal savings account. You need to keep track of how much money you have in the bank. If you have more than $100,000, you need to spread your money over several banks to ensure safety. Keep tabs on your accounts to make sure they don't go over the limit.

Social Security Alert

Congress has been working on a Social Security reform bill intended to keep the program solvent into the 21st century. Currently, senior citizens with incomes above $44,000 have as much as 85% of their benefits taxed. Congress is looking into having this 85% rule apply to Social Security recipients who earn even less. I think it's safe to assume that *if* you get a Social Security check in the next century, it probably will be smaller than the current payouts.

Check Your FICA

You or your accountant should check your FICA account. FICA stands for the Federal Insurance Contribution Act, the legislation that established Social Security during the Great Depression and the administration of Franklin Roosevelt. Your FICA account was established to set money aside for you as you get older.

During the FDR administration, Social Security was seen as the foundation for a good retirement plan. Although many Americans still think that Social Security will be their primary source of income at retirement, the program was never intended to provide more than 25% of the money you need for your retirement. For almost all retired people these days, the $13,000 maximum Social Security benefit does not even come close to paying the bills. Assuming the system continues to make payouts at the present rate, it's likely that benefits will continue to decrease, while inflation continues to increase.

This change impacts you if you plan to continue working after you retire. Recently, workers could have extra working income of only about $8,000 per year before their Social Security benefits would be cut. Only after age 70 can you work without getting a cut in benefits.

FICA is the most elusive of all taxes because you never even see the money that is being credited toward your Social Security. You will need these credits to get benefits at retirement. As if paying the tax isn't bad enough, there's a chance that you aren't being credited properly. Many people find errors in their Social Security reports. And don't assume that all that money will be available when you retire. With the present state of government finances, Congress is constantly raiding the Social Security fund to come up with extra cash.

You can believe that Murphy's Law applies to the government— anything that can go wrong will go wrong. Your FICA account is subject to an almost infinite number of errors. Companies move, merge, are sold, change their names, and go out of business every day. Any or all of these occurrences can cause your records to be lost. Women who interrupt their careers to have children are particularly likely to have mistakes in their records. Also, part-time workers may not have their hours properly credited.

Compounding the problem is the fact that the government's record-keeping system is antiquated and incapable of monitoring records of the 100 million workers they keep track of at any given time. The government has acknowledged numerous problems, but that doesn't help you. You still need to fight the bureaucracy and try to resolve the mistakes in your favor.

To determine whether your account is accurate, you need to fill out form SSA-7004, which you can obtain from the Social Security Administration office. A few weeks after you mail the form, you will receive a report from the SSA detailing all credits on your file. If you find an error, report it to the SSA and have all the necessary documentation to back it up.

You should file a form every couple of years to stay on top of your credits. If you are self-employed, be doubly diligent in checking because you're paying double the FICA rate. The IRS sees you as the employer and employee. Keep tabs on your account if you want what is rightfully due to you at retirement.

ACTION LIST:

1. Check with your benefits department or person in charge of benefits to find out what retirement options are available to you. Take full advantage of every plan they offer.

   Date completed: _____

2. If you haven't started saving for retirement yet, start today by opening an IRA account with a no-load mutual fund company. Even $50 would be a great start.

   Date completed: _____

3. Look into the option of investing in a variable annuity for further tax-deferred savings.

   Date completed: _____

4. Diversify your assets according to your age as described in this chapter. This model will give you stability in good and bad times.

   Date completed: _____

—A Special Offer—

HOW TO HAVE THE $ENSIBLE $AVER'S BLOCKBUSTER ADVICE EVERY MONTH FOR ONLY 6 CENTS PER DAY!!

If you crave even more fresh advice from *The Sensible Saver*, how about subscribing to the monthly newsletter? Every eight-page newsletter is packed with new and exciting money-saving tips and strategies to help you save hundreds. Sign up today and receive a special savings just because you were kind enough to buy this book. **Not** subscribing could be hazardous to your wealth! Call **1-800-231-1994** today.

$ensible $aver Publications, Inc.
6488 Victory Drive
Acworth, Georgia 30102
email: mmiller@sensiblesaver.com
Visit our World Wide Web site at
http://www.sensiblesaver.com

The $ensible $aver Special Offer
Subscription Form

___ YES! YES! YES! I'm anxious to save hundreds more dollars right away. Sign me up for one year, 12 monthly issues of *The $ensible $aver* at the special rate of only $24.95. I'll save $5 off the regular rate of $29.95! **I understand there is no risk to me** because if I am not completely satisfied with the newsletter for any reason, I'm entitled to a complete refund, no questions asked.

___ YES! YES! YES! I want an even better deal. Sign me up for two years, 24 monthly issues for only $44.95. I'll save even more; $15 off the regular rate of $59.95!

(Please print)

Name: _____

Phone: _____

Address: _____ City: _____

State: ____ ZIP: _____

Please charge my ___Visa ___Mastercard ___American Express ___Discover

the amount from above: $_____

Card #: _____

Exp. Date: _____

Signature: _____

___ I have enclosed my check or money order made payable to $ensible $aver Publications, Inc., 6488 Victory Drive, Acworth, Georgia, 30102.

For the fastest service, call **1-800-231-1994** to use your credit card.

INDEX

W